William Wordsworth

The Pedlar
Tintern Abbey
THE TWO-PART PRELUDE

D1110771

William Wordsworth

The Pedlar
Tintern Abbey
THE TWO-PART PRELUDE

Edited with a critical introduction and notes by
Jonathan Wordsworth

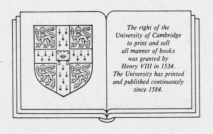

The right of the
University of Cambridge
to print and sell
all manner of books
was granted by
Henry VIII in 1534.
The University has printed
and published continuously
since 1584.

Cambridge University Press

Cambridge
London   New York   New Rochelle
Melbourne   Sydney

Contents

Introduction   *page* 1

Texts   *The Pedlar*   19

          Tintern Abbey   33

          The Two-Part *Prelude*   41

Note on texts

The texts in this volume are those prepared for the forthcoming Cambridge *Wordsworth*, and I am grateful to the Trustees of Dove Cottage for permission to print from manuscripts at the Wordsworth Library, Grasmere. Original spelling has been retained; ampersands have been eliminated; and in words that are no longer likely to be mispronounced, apostrophe 'd' has been replaced by the normal 'ed'. Initial capital letters, which in the manuscripts (and in general among Wordsworth's contemporaries) are frequent but inconsistent, have been retained only for 'God' and 'Nature'.

Published by the Press Syndicate of the University of Cambridge
The Pitt Building, Trumpington Street, Cambridge CB2 1RP
32 East 57th Street, New York, NY 10022, USA
10 Stamford Road, Oakleigh, Melbourne 3166, Australia

© Jonathan Wordsworth 1985

First published 1985

Printed in Great Britain at the University Press, Cambridge

Library of Congress catalogue card number: 84 – 12126

British Library Cataloguing in Publication Data
Wordsworth, William, *1770–1850*
The Pedlar, Tintern Abbey and The Two-Part
Prelude.
I. Title   II. Wordsworth, Jonathan
821'.7   PR5852
ISBN 0 521 26526 6 hard covers
ISBN 0 521 31937 4 paperback

WD

Introduction

Readers of Wordsworth's great autobiographical poem, *The Prelude*, must very often have wished it was shorter. Few can have been aware that the poet had at one stage written a version covering the most important periods of his life, childhood and adolescence, in under a thousand lines. The two-Part *Prelude* (*1799*) is an independent and beautifully self-contained work, which not only includes most of the famous poetry that has become known through later forms of the poem, but presents the great sequences – the 'spots of time'[1] especially – in their original and most striking combination. Wordsworth did not himself publish any version of *The Prelude*, but he worked on the poem intermittently for more than forty years. His final text, made neater but on the whole weakened by revision, was published by his executors in 1850. Seventy-six years later, Ernest de Selincourt printed from the manuscripts the earliest of the full-length *Preludes*, belonging to 1805; first publication of the original two-Part poem was delayed till 1973.[2] In the present volume the text completed in 1799 is offered for the first time in a separate and annotated edition. For the convenience of the reader, it is prefaced by similarly annotated texts of the two poems that form a natural introduction: *The Pedlar* and *Tintern Abbey*, both of 1798.

The beginnings of Wordsworth's great philosophical poetry can be dated very accurately to February 1798. The poet had moved with his sister Dorothy to Alfoxden in Somerset to be close to Coleridge, who was living in the nearby village of Nether Stowey. The previous summer, Wordsworth had composed his great narrative poem, *The Ruined Cottage*, and in November Coleridge had written two of his most famous works, *Kubla Khan* and *The Ancient Mariner*.[3] Both men were

---

[1] Childhood memories that had particular importance for Wordsworth; discussed below, pp. 10–13.

[2] It was first published in *The Poems of William Wordsworth*, selected and ed. Jonathan Wordsworth, Limited Editions Club (Cambridge, 1973). Since then it has appeared in *The Norton Anthology of English Literature* and been edited with photographs and transcripts of the manuscript by Stephen Parrish as a volume in the Cornell Wordsworth Series (Ithaca, N.Y., 1977). Most recently it has appeared in the Norton Critical Edition of *The Prelude, 1799, 1805, 1850*, ed. Jonathan Wordsworth, M.H.Abrams and Stephen Gill (New York, 1979).

[3] Both *The Ruined Cottage* and *The Ancient Mariner* existed at this stage in short versions that have not been preserved.

suddenly writing at their very best – as indeed was Dorothy, whose *Alfoxden Journal* tells us so much about the life they were all living, and the materials out of which the poetry was being made. *The Pedlar*, composed by Wordsworth in February, was designed to go into *The Ruined Cottage*; and though it is the poet's first autobiographical work – and sections of it were later included in *The Prelude* – it is written in the third person. In writing a life-history for the narrator of Margaret's tragic story, Wordsworth makes use of his own experience not just because it comes readily to mind, but because he now sees *The Ruined Cottage* as a way of expressing new philosophical views he has taken over from Coleridge.

Coleridge was a Unitarian; in fact in January 1798 he had applied for a job as a minister. Following the great scientist and founder of modern Unitarianism, Joseph Priestley, he denied the doctrine of the Trinity, believing instead that Christ was the son of Joseph and an ordinary man. The positive aspect of this belief, which is to be found in a succession of Coleridge poems of the period, and which inspired the Wordsworth of *The Pedlar* and *Tintern Abbey*, was that God is present in the natural world as a pervasive life-force,

> A motion and a spirit that impels
> All thinking things, all objects of all thought,
> And rolls through all things.
>   (*Tintern Abbey*, 101–3)

To Coleridge, and to the Wordsworth of early 1798, it seemed that God's presence could actually be perceived in Nature:

> in all things
> He saw one life, and felt that it was joy.
>   (*Pedlar*, 217–18)

The Pedlar was created by Wordsworth as an ideal – a man fully responsive to the One Life, and therefore responsive also to his fellow men. Looking back, it seemed to the poet that his own upbringing among the lakes and mountains of Cumbria had been especially favoured, and childhood is offered in his poem not just as a period of especial happiness, but as the source of adult strength and security:

> He many an evening to his distant home
> In solitude returning saw the hills
> Grow larger in the darkness, all alone
> Beheld the stars come out above his head,
> And travelled through the wood, no comrade near
> To whom he might confess the things he saw.
>   So the foundations of his mind were laid.
> In such communion, not from terror free,
> While yet a child, and long before his time,

> He had perceived the presence and the power
> Of greatness . . .
>   (*Pedlar*, 20–30)

It is interesting to put beside this very early piece of Wordsworth autobiographical poetry, a passage from *Frost at Midnight*, the poem that Coleridge was writing in the same month. He too is thinking about childhood and the formative influence of the One Life, but his terms are more evidently Christian:

>   thou, my babe, shalt wander like a breeze
> By lakes and sandy shores, beneath the crags
> Of ancient mountain . . .
>   so shalt thou see and hear
> The lovely shapes and sounds intelligible
> Of that eternal language which thy God
> Utters, who from eternity doth teach
> Himself in all, and all things in himself.
>   (*Frost at Midnight*, 54–62)

The two poets were influencing each other in everything they wrote. Coleridge, who had at this stage scarcely been near a lake or ancient mountain, is to be seen wishing for his son, Hartley, the landscape of a Wordsworthian childhood; Wordsworth meanwhile confers upon the child Pedlar (effectively upon his own earlier self) a form of communion with the One Life. At times the views that Wordsworth holds at this period do find expression in terms of God, but he seems to have taken over Coleridge's Unitarianism in a very undoctrinal way, almost as if it were the confirmation of something he instinctively believed. Coleridge as philosopher and theologian was trying to understand (often in scientific terms that now seem crazy) how it was that a God who was all spirit could be present in the solid matter that composes the universe.[1] Wordsworth's focus was quite different. He too was looking for an explanation, but it was for his own sense of the numinous, his experience that in certain exalted moods the individual is capable of reaching out beyond the boundaries of the self.[2]

The Pedlar and *Tintern Abbey* have it in common that they offer these models as mystical experience, a loss of bodily awareness, and merging of the self into a total harmony that is love, or joy, or God. Looking out over the coastline at sunrise, the Pedlar responds to the sea and the landscape as sharing his own 'gladness and deep joy' – or

---

[1] Priestley's experiments led, for instance, to speculation that God might be present as electricity, charging the apparently lifeless material world.
[2] For discussion of these moods, see Jonathan Wordsworth, *The Borders of Vision* (Oxford, 1982).

perhaps it is that he is sharing theirs:

> The ocean and the earth beneath him lay
> In gladness and deep joy. The clouds were touched,
> And in their silent faces did he read
> Unutterable love. Sound needed none,
> Nor any voice of joy: his spirit drank
> The spectacle. Sensation, soul, and form,
> All melted into him; they swallowed up
> His animal being. In them did he live,
> And by them did he live – they were his life.
> In such access of mind, in such high hour
> Of visitation from the living God,
> He did not feel the God, he felt his works.
> Thought was not; in enjoyment it expired.
> Such hour by prayer or praise was unprofaned;
> He neither prayed, nor offered thanks or praise;
> His mind was a thanksgiving to the power
> That made him. It was blessedness and love.
>
> (*Pedlar*, 98–114)

There is an interchanging of roles that goes on throughout the passage, as the Pedlar's feelings are either conferred upon, or felt to be present in, the external world. The clouds seem human not only in their silent faces, but in being 'touched', responsive; and the Pedlar receives back his own sensation as a gift. Most strange and powerful of all these exchanges is the 'access of mind'. It is as though mind has become a quality beyond the self, and the poet raises his verse to a new rhetorical level in describing the experience as a 'high hour / Of visitation from the living God'. What follows is quite unexpected. God, who has seemed to have the full support of Christian tradition as he carries out his impressive polysyllabic 'visitation', is suddenly diminished in a line of monosyllables that take from him all grandeur and personal authority: 'He did not feel the God, he felt his works'. The definite article seems especially belittling – to be '*the* God', as opposed to God himself, is well on the way to being merely *a* god. Power is transferred from the Creator to his creation; and as a part of this, the Pedlar gives thanks not through the time-honoured rituals of prayer and praise, but simply in the act of response. Like the clouds he is touched, and the love that he reads in their faces is the sensation – the blessing and the blessedness – of his own mind.

Important as the *Pedlar* lines are, they are rather inaccessible as poetry. We are conscious all the time of being presented with an ideal. Wordsworth's tones seem needlessly emphatic (the heavy assonance and alliteration of 'Such hour by prayer or praise was unprofaned' is the extreme example), and the verse because it is made up of so many individually impressive statements lacks the fluency that would draw us in. The comparable passage in *Tintern Abbey* is far more persuasive. With the help of Coleridge's Conversation Poems, *Frost at Midnight* especially, Wordsworth has found a way of making the big assertions, and yet staying on a personal level. Instead of poetry that describes a state of mind, he offers now the perfect evocation of a mood, achieved through a building up of rhythms that enforce and complement the claims that are being made.

> Nor less, I trust,
> To them I may have owed another gift,
> Of aspect more sublime: that blessed mood
> In which the burthen of the mystery,
> In which the heavy and the weary weight
> Of all this unintelligible world,
> Is lightened – that serene and blessed mood
> In which the affections gently lead us on,
> Until, the breath of this corporeal frame
> And even the motion of our human blood
> Almost suspended, we are laid asleep
> In body and become a living soul,
> While, with an eye made quiet by the power
> Of harmony and the deep power of joy,
> We see into the life of things.
>
> (*Tintern Abbey*, 36–50)

Perhaps the most remarkable thing about this great passage – aside from the sheer quality of the writing – is the situation in which the poet's mood has been experienced. Wordsworth under his dark sycamore in early July 1798 is not responding directly to the 'steep and lofty cliffs' and other features of the Wye Valley above Tintern Abbey; he is recalling a response made, at different times and in different places, to a landscape of the mind – a peculiarly vivid memory that had been stored up from an earlier visit to the scene that is now in front of him. That Wordsworth placed an unusual importance on visual memory is shown as early as September 1790 when he comments to Dorothy on the beauty of the Alps: 'perhaps scarce a day of my life will pass in which I shall not derive some happiness from these images'.[1] Storing up images (mental pictures) seems at times to have been almost a conscientious process; but of course it worked because of the strength of the poet's original emotion. Once again it is *The Pedlar* that offers the most useful insights. 'Deep feelings',

---

[1] To Dorothy Wordsworth, 6 September 1790; *Letters of William and Dorothy Wordsworth: The Early Years, 1787–1805* ('*EY*' in future references), revised by Chester L. Shaver (Oxford, 1967), p. 36.

Wordsworth writes,

> had impressed
> Great objects on his mind with portraiture
> And colour so distinct that on his mind
> They lay like substances, and almost seemed
> To haunt the bodily sense . . .
>
> he thence attained
> An *active* power to fasten images
> Upon his brain, and on their pictured lines
> Intensely brooded, even till they acquired
> The liveliness of dreams.
>
> (*Pedlar*, 30–4, 39–43; Wordsworth's italics)

If one thinks of the various stages of this process in the case of *Tintern Abbey*, the story begins in August 1793 when Wordsworth in an exhausted state of mind first encountered the Wye Valley, having walked largely without food across Salisbury Plain. Either deliberately using his '*active* power to fasten images / Upon his brain', or simply as the result of an emotional response to the scenery, he carries away with him especially vivid memories. In their strange tangibility, these are felt to 'haunt the bodily sense', just as 'the sounding cataract' is said to have haunted the poet 'like a passion' (*Tintern Abbey*, 77–8) at the time of his original visit. Fascinated by the clarity of the Tintern memories, the mind returns to them again and again in the years that follow, brooding over them in a process that creates for them the imaginative quality of a dream. At all periods in Wordsworth's life such recollections were a source of delight – the daffodils, for instance, that he and Dorothy had seen on Ullswater in April 1802 are said two years later to 'flash upon that inward eye / Which is the bliss of solitude' (*Daffodils*, 15–16) – but only in *Tintern Abbey* does he make the extraordinary claim that images of Nature within the mind can lead to a mystical perception of God.

Perhaps the belief in the One Life was too exalted to last, or maybe it needed to be sustained by companionship with the Unitarian Coleridge; at all events, extreme pantheist claims of this kind, though they do appear elsewhere in Wordsworth's poetry, are typical only of his stay near Coleridge at Alfoxden in the first half of 1798. When he begins work on the two-Part *Prelude* in the autumn, the poet and Dorothy are at Goslar in Germany, and away from any direct influence. His new poem shows him to be still preoccupied with memory, and with the effect of Nature on the human mind, but he is interested now in different, less tranquil, forms of experience, and he is looking for different kinds of explanation. Taking up a notebook later used by Dorothy for one of her *Journals*, Wordsworth asks himself a series of questions: '*Was it for this* . . . ? *For this didst thou,* / *O Derwent* . . . ? Beloved

Derwent, fairest of all streams, / *Was it for this* . . . ?' Already, it seems, he is worried at his failure to get on with writing *The Recluse*, the great philosophical work which had been planned with Coleridge in the spring, and which would in fact never be completed.[1] How could he explain his present apathy when the childhood that he looked back on had seemed to promise so much?

It is clear from the notebook that the two-Part *Prelude* had not been planned. It began because Wordsworth allowed his mind to play over one or two early memories that had come to seem specially important:

> 'twas my joy
> To wander half the night among the cliffs
> And the smooth hollows where the woodcocks ran
> Along the moonlight turf . . .
>
> Oh, when I have hung
> Above the raven's nest, by knots of grass
> Or half-inch fissures in the slippery rock
> But ill sustained, and almost, as it seemed,
> Suspended by the blast which blew amain,
> Shouldering the naked crag . . .
> (*1799*, I. 30–3, 57–62)

As well as their vividness, the memories have in common the presence of fear. Like the boy Pedlar who 'travelled through the wood, no comrade near / To whom he might confess the things he saw' (ll. 24–5), the child is in almost all these episodes frightened at his solitude. Suspended above the raven's nest he experiences a sort of awe – 'With what strange utterance did the loud dry wind / Blow through my ears' (I. 64–5) – and the woodcock-snaring episode ends with still more positive menace:

> and when the deed was done
> I heard among the solitary hills
> Low breathings coming after me, and sounds
> Of undistinguishable motion, steps
> Almost as silent as the turf they trod.
> (I. 45–9)

Though as readers we know that the child's fears are imaginary (produced on this occasion by guilt at having stolen a woodcock from somebody else's snare), we are invited to enter into his mind, experience with him the sense of a punishing supernatural presence. More surprisingly we are also asked to regard his experience as formative, beneficial, evidence that the poet had been from the first 'a chosen son'

[1] For an account of Wordsworth's forty years of hope and disappointment over *The Recluse*, see *The Borders of Vision*, Epilogue, 'The Light That Never Was'.

(*Pedlar*, 326). 'The mind of man', Wordsworth writes impressively,

> is fashioned and built up
> Even as a strain of music. I believe
> That there are spirits which, when they would form
> A favored being, from his very dawn
> Of infancy do open out the clouds
> As at the touch of lightning, seeking him
> With gentle visitation . . .
> (I. 67–73)

The placing of 'I believe' alone at the end of a line sounds very much like the beginning of a Creed, and in Wordsworth's mind the spirits he refers to must be related to the One Life of *The Pedlar* and *Tintern Abbey* which he had certainly taken seriously. Their being in the plural, though, makes them seem more literary, and they don't really seem very different from the guardian-spirits who appear in so many eighteenth-century poems merely as decoration. Wordsworth's purpose, however, is clear. The spirits represent forces that he believes to have been at work in his childhood, and they enable him to distinguish between formative influences that were gentle in their effect, and the harsher kinds of experience that seemed in his case to have been more important:

> Others too there are, who use,
> Yet haply aiming at the self-same end,
> Severer interventions, ministry
> More palpable – and of their school was I.
> (I. 77–80)

Wordsworth is not just talking about happy and unhappy childhood experiences. There is an odd mixture of tenderness and power even in the image he chooses of 'gentle visitation' – 'the *touch* of lightning' – and however one may react to the literariness of the spirit world, what the poet's language ('use', 'aiming', 'end', 'interventions', 'ministry', 'school') is stressing again and again is his sense of having been positively singled out. Five years later, in the beautiful *Intimations Ode* (1802–4), he goes so far as to give thanks for the guilts and terrors he has had to put up with as a child – the 'blank misgivings of a creature / Moving about in worlds not realized' (ll. 142–3).

As a climax to the 'severer interventions' that make up the first section of *1799*, Part I, Wordsworth offers the episode of the stolen boat. Rowing out onto Ullswater by night, the child fixes his eye on the ridge that forms the horizon, and is startled by the sudden appearance of a larger, more distant, crag as he gets further from the shore.[1] In these terms it all seems very simple, but for the child it had been a

---

[1] For diagram, see note to *1799*, I. 107–10.

moment of 'blank misgiving', and the experience draws from Wordsworth some of his finest poetry:

> twenty times
> I dipped my oars into the silent lake,
> And as I rose upon the stroke my boat
> Went heaving through the water like a swan –
> When from behind that rocky steep, till then
> The bound of the horizon, a huge cliff,
> As if with voluntary power instinct,
> Upreared its head. I struck, and struck again,
> And, growing still in stature, the huge cliff
> Rose up between me and the stars, and still,
> With measured motion, like a living thing
> Strode after me. With trembling hands I turned,
> And through the silent water stole my way
> Back to the cavern of the willow-tree.
>
> (I. 103–16)

Wordsworth's sense of what it was like to be the child – first proud of his swan-like boat, then terrified by the motion that his own rowing has imparted to the cliff, then stealing guilty through the silent water – is exceptionally strong. On this occasion he takes us beyond the experience and its immediate effects, and into the mind that 'works' (like the swell of the sea) 'with a dim and undetermined sense / Of unknown modes of being':

> In my thoughts
> There was a darkness – call it solitude,
> Or blank desertion – no familiar shapes
> Of hourly objects, images of trees,
> Of sea or sky, no colours of green fields,
> But huge and mighty forms that do not live
> Like living men moved slowly through my mind
> By day, and were the trouble of my dreams.
>
> (I. 121–9)

Rising up between him and the stars (which have been a reassuring natural presence), the mountain deprives the child of 'the ballast of familiar life' (*1805*, VII. 604) – images of dependable ordinary things that have been impressed on his mind as in *The Pedlar*. He has lost his sense of actuality, become indeed 'a creature / Moving about in worlds not realized'. Worse still is the new 'moving about' that is going on within the world of his mind – a slow torture as the mountain possesses his imagination, striding through the internal solitude with a 'measured motion' that gives it life, but gives it also the terrible power of the automaton.

At this stage in the two-Part *Prelude* readers of the 1805 and 1850 texts will have noticed that the long introduction to Book I has yet to be written, but may have seen few other differences. In *1799*, however – and only in *1799* – the episodes that have so far been discussed are balanced by a further series: the great 'spots of time' sequence, which in *1805* is moved from its original place, one episode going to Book V, the other two to Book XI[1]. The result of moving the sequence was not merely to weaken Book I in later versions of the poem, but to destroy a very important progression of thought. The memories that lead up to the stealing of the boat show in the child an imaginative response that is valued by the adult poet both for its vividness, and because it seems to justify his feelings of having been singled out; but no links are made between past and present. In the 'spots of time', written two or three months later at the beginning of 1799, Wordsworth goes on to suggest a positive continuity within the mind. Childhood experience is not just interesting to look back on, it is the source of the poet's strength at the time of writing:

> There are in our existence spots of time
> Which with distinct preeminence retain
> A fructifying virtue, whence, depressed
> By trivial occupations and the round
> Of ordinary intercourse, our minds –
> Especially the imaginative power –
> Are nourished and invisibly repaired.
> Such moments chiefly seem to have their date
> In our first childhood.
>
> (I. 288–96)

In the background is *Tintern Abbey*: once again Wordsworth is talking about a process that lightens 'the heavy and the weary weight / Of all this unintelligible world' (ll. 40–2). And once again the process works through the tendency of the mind to go back to memories that have achieved a special importance. In *Tintern Abbey*, however, the memories had been of landscape, and had led to a mystical seeing into the life of things; now they are of personal experience, and the mind acknowledges no power beyond its own. The new claims ought to be less impressive, but Wordsworth himself doesn't seem to think them so. For the first time in his writings he has become preoccupied with his own creativity. The memories that concern him have a 'fructifying virtue' – a power to make the writer fruitful.

No kind of justice can be done to the 'spots of time' in a brief account. The sequence as a whole, 114 lines in its original form, must be among the two or three greatest passages of blank verse that

---

[1] *1799*, I. 258–79 become *1805*, V. 45–73, and I. 288–374 are revised and extended to form *1805*, XI. 257–388.

Wordsworth ever wrote. In *1799* it opens with the discovery of the
drowned man on Esthwaite Water (later *1805*, v. 450–73). Like the
mountain that rises up between the child and the stars, he rises 'bolt
upright . . . with his ghastly face', a shocking intrusion into the
'beauteous scene / Of trees and hills and water' and natural harmony
(1. 277–9). Most obviously it is death that he brings into the poetry, but
in more general ways too he prepares us for the concept of the 'spot of
time', and for the two extended episodes that are to follow. The first
of these, the scene near the murderer's gibbet at Penrith, is much
revised in *1805*, and shows in its original form a strength and simplicity
that later gets lost among the details of local superstition:

> I remember well . . .
> While I was as yet an urchin, one who scarce
> Could hold a bridle, with ambitious hopes
> I mounted, and we rode towards the hills.
> We were a pair of horsemen: honest James
> Was with me, my encourager and guide.
>
> (*1799*, 1. 296–303)

The poet's tones express a gentle mockery of his former self, and at the
same time catch the child's own fantasy of setting out with his squire
on a quest. James in reality was his grandparents' servant, and the
child himself would probably have been five. It is important to
remember as one reads this poetry that Wordsworth had no regard for
facts in their own right. His autobiography is a life of the mind, and the
childhood experiences are least of all likely to be the record of particular occasions:

> We had not travelled long ere some mischance
> Disjoined me from my comrade, and, through fear
> Dismounting, down the rough and stony moor
> I led my horse, and stumbling on, at length
> Came to a bottom where in former times
> A man, the murderer of his wife, was hung
> In irons. Mouldered was the gibbet-mast;
> The bones were gone, the iron and the wood;
> Only a long green ridge of turf remained
> Whose shape was like a grave.
>
> (*1799*, 1. 304–13)

'I left the spot', Wordsworth continues, and in this original version of
the passage we read straight on with no cluttering detail into the
strange and beautiful vision of the woman on the hill:

> I left the spot,
> And reascending the bare slope I saw
> A naked pool that lay beneath the hills,
> The beacon on the summit, and more near

> A girl who bore a pitcher on her head
> And seemed with difficult steps to force her way
> Against the blowing wind. It was in truth
> An ordinary sight, but I should need
> Colours and words that are unknown to man
> To paint the visionary dreariness
> Which, while I looked all round for my lost guide,
> Did at that time invest the naked pool,
> The beacon on the lonely eminence,
> The woman and her garments vexed and tossed
> By the strong wind.
>
> (*1799*, I. 313–27)

By chance we know that Wordsworth in the early part of his account is conflating two murder stories, or at least recalling two different gibbets: a recent gallows near Penrith Beacon, which was still standing at the time of the *Prelude* episode, but which there is no reason to think the poet ever saw; and another at Hawkshead, which had indeed belonged to 'A man, the murderer of his wife', and which had mouldered to a terrifying stump that he passed every day on his way to school. What is happening, though, is more subtle than a mere combining of stories and selecting of details. Wordsworth is creating for the reader an atmosphere in which the numinous unexplained appearance of the woman on the hill will have its fullest effect. At the same time he is suggesting how within the mind of the child the original experience came to take on such importance. In both reader and child, the background presence of horror heightens and intensifies response, investing the landscape, and the woman who is its central focus, with a vividness that they could not ordinarily possess. We tend to think of this as an incident, but of course nothing happens. In terms of *The Pedlar*, what we have is another visual image impressed upon the mind by fear and isolation; only this time there is a human being at its centre. And also, there is motion – not very much, but it is extremely important that the girl with the pitcher on her head is winning her battle against the wind that vexes and tosses her garments. If she were static she would be merely a picture; as it is, she lives on in the imagination of countless readers, as she had lived on in the poet's own.

In a quite different way, the final 'spot of time' is equally impressive. Again Wordsworth is concerned with the power of mind to invest a landscape with significance, but he has moved on now from recreating what might originally have been felt, to thinking about the strange effects of memory. Waiting for horses that will take him and his brothers home for the Christmas holidays, the boy sits 'half sheltered by a naked wall':

Upon my right hand was a single sheep,
A whistling hawthorn on my left, and there,
Those two companions at my side, I watched
With eyes intensely straining . . .

(I. 343–7)

The use of the word 'companions' seems almost facetious; one feels
that nothing could give importance to such an unpromising collection
of objects as a wall, a sheep, and a hawthorn bush. It is guilt that does
so. The child has been home only a few days when his father dies.
Remembering how he had looked forward to the holidays, he feels that
he has been punished – in effect, that he has caused his father's death
– and the guilty recollections of his hope give to the remembered scene
the same visionary quality of desolation experienced in the previous
'spot'. This time, though, the poet goes on to make the claim that both
the 'spots' are intended to support – that such memories will not only
acquire and retain a 'distinct preeminence', but are the source of
future imaginative power:

And afterwards the wind and sleety rain,
And all the business of the elements,
The single sheep, and the one blasted tree,
And the bleak music of that old stone wall . . .
All these were spectacles and sounds to which
I often would repair, and thence would drink
As at a fountain. And I do not doubt
That in this later time, when storm and rain
Beat on my roof at midnight, or by day
When I am in the woods, unknown to me
The workings of my spirit thence are brought.

(I. 361–4, 368–74)

The first three episodes of Part I (the 'severer interventions', I. I–
129) belong to October–November 1798, the second major group (the
'spots of time', I. 258–374) seems to have been composed in January
1799. Between the two sequences, Wordsworth wrote the great
skating scene (I. 150–85), probably not at first intending it for his new
poem. In autumn 1799, however, when the two-Part *Prelude* was taking
its final shape, he appears to have decided that there ought to be some
emphasis on normal happy experience in his account of childhood. He
inserted the 'home amusements' section (I. 206–33) – partly successful
in its mock-heroic imitation of card-games in Pope and Cowper,[1]
partly rather feeble – and he introduced the skating scene to form the
only 'gentle visitation' of Part I. In general one might expect the
'ministry more palpable' of terror, guilt, pain, to produce the greater

[1] See note to *1799*, I. 208–12, below.

poetry, but this is a passage that can stand comparison even with the stealing of the boat and the two major 'spots of time':

> All shod with steel
> We hissed along the polished ice in games
> Confederate, imitative of the chace
> And woodland pleasures, the resounding horn,
> The pack loud bellowing, and the hunted hare.
> So through the darkness and the cold we flew,
> And not a voice was idle. With the din,
> Meanwhile, the precipices rang aloud;
> The leafless trees and every icy crag
> Tinkled like iron; while the distant hills
> Into the tumult sent an alien sound
> Of melancholy, not unnoticed; while the stars,
> Eastward, were sparkling clear, and in the west
> The orange sky of evening died away.
>
> (I. 156–69)

At first it seems that this is to be an example of the 'glad animal movements' and 'coarser pleasures' of Wordsworth's boyish days (*Tintern Abbey*, 74–5); but the unthinking din with which the skaters ward off the darkness and the cold cannot protect them entirely from the kind of larger awareness that will question the value of their games. Indeed the din actually causes both the iron tinkling of the trees and crags, and the echoes from the distant hills that intrude upon the consciousness, bringing with them what Wordsworth so beautifully calls 'an alien sound / Of melancholy'. Responsive to this call to thoughtfulness, the poet chooses solitude, leaving the pack for the pleasure of skating alone into a silent bay, or stopping suddenly short to feel the imaginative experience of being at the still point of the turning world:

> And oftentimes
> When we had given our bodies to the wind,
> And all the shadowy banks on either side
> Came sweeping through the darkness, spinning still
> The rapid line of motion, then at once
> Have I, reclining back upon my heels,
> Stopped short – yet still the solitary cliffs
> Wheeled by me, even as if the earth had rolled
> With visible motion her diurnal round.
> Behind me did they stretch in solemn train,
> Feebler and feebler, and I stood and watched
> Till all was tranquil as a summer sea.
>
> (I. 174–85)

There is no doubt that adolescence, the subject of Part II of the 1799

Prelude, was less important to Wordsworth than childhood. He did not feel it to have been in the same way a source of adult powers, and his memories of the period did not apparently contain the guilts and terrors that he associated with the most heightened moments of child-hood vision. The stress on education continues in his account of adolescence, but (to use the famous distinction made by Edmund Burke) where Nature in Part I had been seen in terms of the sublime, Part II is concerned with the beautiful.[1] Superficially the visit to the ruins of Furness Abbey in Part II may seem very like the skating episode. Once again an account of shared physical pleasure (this time in horsemanship) comes to its high point in a moment of solitary imaginative experience. Listening to the wren, however, 'Which one day sang so sweetly in the nave / Of the old church' (II. 122–3), the poet is completely unthreatened. The 'alien sound of melancholy', sublime in its refusal to be a party to human pleasures, has been replaced by a song that is utterly harmonious. The boy's relation to his companions too has changed. He is no longer an outsider; his responsiveness is no longer of a kind that could not be shared – if anything it seems to enhance the general happiness:

> though from recent showers
> The earth was comfortless, and, touched by faint
> Internal breezes, from the roofless walls
> The shuddering ivy dripped large drops, yet still
> So sweetly mid the gloom the invisible bird
> Sang to itself that there I could have made
> My dwelling-place, and lived for ever there,
> To hear such music. Through the walls we flew
> And down the valley, and, a circuit made
> In wantonness of heart, through rough and smooth
> We scampered homeward.
>
> (II. 123–33)

It is typical of Wordsworth, who was no more interested in chron-ology than in other kinds of fact, that the central question he asks in the section of his poem given to adolescence should take him back beyond the childhood experiences of Part I. The 'spots of time' had left a question that needed to be answered – how was it that the child came in the first place to possess an imagination that could transform his surroundings, and lead forward to future restoration? 'Who that shall point as with a wand', Wordsworth writes half-way through Part II,

[1] The influence of Burke's *Philosophical Enquiry into the Origin of our Ideas of the Sub-lime and Beautiful* (1757) is to be seen in both Wordsworth and Coleridge – and indeed in almost all late eighteenth-century writing about landscape and response.

> and say
> 'This portion of the river of my mind
> Came from yon fountain'?
> (II. 247–9)

He is not prepared to attempt such magic himself, but he goes on to speculate about infancy, and the relationship of mother and child, in a way that shows him to have been a hundred years ahead of his time. The infant he sees as holding 'mute dialogues' with his mother's heart (II. 313), 'gather[ing] passion from his mother's eye' (II. 273). Her 'feelings pass into his torpid life / Like an awakening breeze', and as a direct result the child acquires the power of ordering and understanding his surroundings (II. 274–80). As one would expect from reading *The Pedlar* and *Tintern Abbey*, the infant's mind is 'Tenacious of the forms which it receives' (II. 284) – already, that is, capable of the Wordsworthian process of storing up visual images – and the link with *Tintern Abbey* becomes still clearer in the lines that follow. In the 'beloved presence' of the mother

> there exists
> A virtue which irradiates and exalts
> All objects through all intercourse of sense.
> (II. 288–90)

In the background one hears unmistakably,

> A motion and spirit that impels
> All thinking things, all objects of all thought . . .
> (*Tintern Abbey*, 101–2)

Asking himself what is the ultimate source of imaginative power, Wordsworth has come up with the answer that for the child objects of the external world are 'irradiated' by the mother's love, just as for the adult they are interfused by the transcendental 'presence' (*Tintern Abbey*, 95) of the One Life. As the *Prelude* account of the Infant Babe develops, the child moves further and further away from 'the babe who sleeps / Upon his mother's breast' (II. 270–1), and becomes more and more obviously a way of talking about human potential:

> From Nature largely he receives, nor so
> Is satisfied, but largely gives again;
> For feeling has to him imparted strength,
> And – powerful in all sentiments of grief,
> Of exultation, fear and joy – his mind,
> Even as an agent of the one great mind,
> Creates, creator and receiver both . . .
> (II. 297–303)

It is not that Wordsworth thinks that an infant *could* be 'powerful in all sentiments of grief, / Of exultation, fear and joy', but that the poetry, after starting with a quite ordinary baby, has moved into a near-

symbolic realm in which the child becomes a type of the fully imaginative mind. It comes as no surprise when Wordsworth adds, 'Such,
verily, is the first / Poetic spirit of our human life' (II. 305–6). In
describing the child as 'creator and receiver both', however, he has
gone beyond the 'poetic', or 'secondary', imagination (as defined by
Coleridge in *Biographia Literaria*, 1817), and made him capable of something very like the godlike 'primary' power, in which creativity and
perception fuse as the individual becomes aware of his true relation to
existence.[1]

The Infant Babe passage is the perfect complement to the 'spots of
time' doctrine in Part I. It is perhaps the greatest strength of the two-
Part *Prelude*, as against later versions of the poem, that Wordsworth's
thinking comes through so much more clearly. Part II is not merely a
continuing of the poet's story into a less vivid time in his life, it is a
highly important extension of his thought. In the final sequences of
the poem two passages written at Alfoxden about the Pedlar are
inserted to show what an adult imaginative vision could, or should,
consist of. The second of these (II. 446–64), including the great
pantheist assertion 'in all things / I saw one life, and felt that it was
joy', comprises *Pedlar*, 204–22 (with the pronoun 'he' changed to 'I');
the first belongs to the same moment at Alfoxden, but seems never to
have been incorporated in a text of *The Pedlar* (or *The Ruined Cottage*). It
is among the most interesting and thoughtful of all Wordsworth's
attempts to define the nature of his inspiration:

> and I would stand
> Beneath some rock, listening to sounds that are
> The ghostly language of the ancient earth,
> Or make their dim abode in distant winds.
> Thence did I drink the visionary power.
> I deem not profitless these fleeting moods
> Of shadowy exaltation; not for this,
> That they are kindred to our purer mind
> And intellectual life, but that the soul –
> Remembering how she felt, but what she felt
> Remembering not – retains an obscure sense

[1]In chapter XIII of *Biographia* Coleridge defines the primary imagination in
magniloquent terms that have often been misunderstood. It may indeed be
that he was frightened by the grandeur of the claim that he was making, and
therefore deliberately imprecise. A simpler definition from chapter XII may
be more useful: 'We proceed from the self, in order to lose and find all self in
GOD.' As in Tintern Abbey, man in his highest creative moments is said to lose
the awareness of an ordinary self, in order to receive back the true self that
can 'see into the life of things'. At one and the same moment he is 'creator and
receiver both'. See note to *1799*, II. 300–5, below.

Of possible sublimity, to which
With growing faculties she doth aspire,
With faculties still growing, feeling still
That whatsoever point they gain they still
Have something to pursue.

(II. 356–71)

With their fluent interchanging rhythms, and their power to make sharp yet sensitive distinctions about the workings of the mind, the lines are immensely impressive; yet they were written earlier than anything in Part I, indeed very probably earlier than anything in *The Pedlar*. In discussing the three poems in this volume it often seems appropriate to emphasize development – a progression that will lead on to still further new poetic voices as the full-length *Prelude* is created in 1804–5. It is useful therefore to have a reminder of continuity and sameness. There is a characteristic Wordsworth to be perceived already in these lines of February 1798, and in the 'obscure sense / Of possible sublimity' he identifies what will prove to be the central preoccupation of his creative life.

It is very important that Wordsworth brings the two-Part *Prelude* to a conclusion with a farewell to Coleridge. Coleridge had at this moment at the end of 1799 decided to go and become a journalist in London (whereas Wordsworth and Dorothy were going to set up house at Dove Cottage in Grasmere), so there was a practical reason for saying goodbye. But there was also a different kind of appropriateness. Wordsworth had been writing throughout with Coleridge in mind. At line 8 of Part I he had quoted from *Frost at Midnight* – Coleridge's own poem about childhood and imagination – and in the conclusion to Part II he inserts another specific reference, thus consciously rounding off the poem and drawing attention to its place in a continuing discussion. Wordsworth never chose a title for *The Prelude*; it was thought of throughout his life as 'The Poem to Coleridge'. For the two-Part version of 1799 the name seems especially appropriate. If *The Pedlar* shows Coleridge's influence at its strongest, and *Tinern Abbey* is the most perfect embodiment of shared beliefs, the two-Part *Prelude* shows Wordsworth inspired by his friend to define his own individuality. In doing so he produced what is now coming to be recognized as one of his very greatest poems.

The Pedlar

Him had I seen the day before, alone
And in the middle of the public way
Standing to rest himself. His eyes were turned
Towards the setting sun, while, with that staff
Behind him fixed, he propped a long white pack
Which crossed his shoulders, wares for maids who live   5
In lonely villages or straggling huts.
I knew him – he was born of lowly race
On Cumbrian hills, and I have seen the tear
Stand in his luminous eye when he described   10
The house in which his early youth was passed,
And found I was no stranger to the spot.
I loved to hear him talk of former days
And tell how when a child, ere yet of age
To be a shepherd, he had learned to read   15
His bible in a school that stood alone,
Sole building on a mountain's dreary edge,
Far from the sight of city spire, or sound
Of minster clock. From that bleak tenement

1   *The Pedlar* starts so abruptly because it was composed, in February–
March 1798, to be inserted in *The Ruined Cottage* (written the previous
summer) and provide a background for the narrator who tells the central tragic story of Margaret. Despite its third-person narrative, it is
Wordsworth's earliest sustained piece of autobiographical and
philosophical writing. Within a year he seems to have decided that it
was too long, or too different, to be part of *The Ruined Cottage*, and in
October 1800 Coleridge refers to it as a separate poem 'entitled *The
Pedlar*', which is to be published with *Christabel*. In 1801–2 *The Pedlar* was
extensively reworked, but it had still not been published when in spring
1804 Wordsworth drew up his scheme for *The Excursion* (published
1814). The Pedlar, rechristened the Wanderer, became in *The Excursion*
the central figure of a long didactic work that was partly narrative,
partly philosophical, and *The Ruined Cottage* in its double-barrelled form
was appropriately used to make the first Book. *The Pedlar* thus lost its
separate identity. It was first published as an independent poem in
1969.
14   **ere** before.
19   **tenement** building.

He many an evening to his distant home
In solitude returning saw the hills
Grow larger in the darkness, all alone
Beheld the stars come out above his head,
And travelled through the wood, no comrade near
To whom he might confess the things he saw.
    So the foundations of his mind were laid.
In such communion, not from terror free,
While yet a child, and long before his time,
He had perceived the presence and the power
Of greatness, and deep feelings had impressed
Great objects on his mind with portraiture
And colour so distinct that on his mind
They lay like substances, and almost seemed
To haunt the bodily sense. He had received
A precious gift, for as he grew in years
With these impressions would he still compare
All his ideal stores, his shapes and forms,
And, being still unsatisfied with aught
Of dimmer character, he thence attained
An *active* power to fasten images
Upon his brain, and on their pictured lines
Intensely brooded, even till they acquired
The liveliness of dreams. Nor did he fail,

27–30 Fear seemed important to Wordsworth as a formative influence because it stimulated the imagination. It is also of course increased by it, as in ll. 19–25. Compare *1799*, I. 67–80.

30–4 Great objects of the natural world are stamped ('impressed') on the child's mind as mental pictures ('images') as the result of strong feelings (of fear, pain, pleasure) that he has experienced in their presence. It is a view that goes back to John Locke (*Essay Concerning Human Understanding*, 1689), but which was known to Coleridge and Wordsworth through David Hartley's *Observations of Man* (1749, republished 1791); see l. 81n, below.

39–43 Memories of actual landscape are valued because they form a standard of comparison for the imaginary ('ideal') scenes that the child has created and stored in his own head. The process by which the mind goes back to remembered landscapes, giving them more and more vividness, was especially important to Wordsworth as a poet. It lies behind the great pantheist claims of *Tintern Abbey*, 23–50, and is celebrated again and again in the two-Part *Prelude* (see, e.g., *1799*, I. 279–94).

42 **even** here scanned as a single syllable, 'e'en' (a poetic usage, but also the pronunciation that Wordsworth would have known as a boy in Cumbria). Compare ll. 51 and 55 below.

While yet a child, with a child's eagerness
Incessantly to turn his ear and eye
On all things which the rolling seasons brought   45
To feed such appetite. Nor this alone
Appeased his yearning – in the after day
Of boyhood, many an hour in caves forlorn
And in the hollow depths of naked crags
He sate, and even in their fixed lineaments,   50
Or from the power of a peculiar eye,
Or by creative feeling overborne,
Or by predominance of thought oppressed,
Even in their fixed and steady lineaments
He traced an ebbing and a flowing mind,   55
Expression ever varying.
                Thus informed,
He had small need of books; for many a tale
Traditionary round the mountains hung,
And many a legend peopling the dark woods   60
Nourished imagination in her growth,
And gave the mind that apprehensive power
By which she is made quick to recognize

51   **sate** the biblical and poetic form of 'sat', but probably like 'e'en' (l. 42) reflecting northern usage.

52–4 **Or . . . Or . . . Or** Either . . . Or . . . Or. The three alternatives that Wordsworth offers – sharpness of personal observation (the 'peculiar eye'), imaginative sympathy, and 'predominance of thought' (thinking so hard as to preclude other forms of response) – are so different that in effect he is saying he doesn't know the cause of the Pedlar's mood. For comparable hesitancy, see ll. 330–44 and *1799*, II, 435–44, below. The verbs 'overborne' (l. 53) and 'oppressed' (l. 54) are important; the moods are uncomfortably intense.

55–7 In his solitary boyhood in Cumbria the Pedlar is not content to see the features ('lineaments') of the landscape as fixed or dead, but traces in them a life-force. Their outward changes (as the result of light, storm, or whatever) become associated with the ebbing and flowing of the mind of God. For the basis of this form of pantheism in Coleridge's reading of Bishop Berkeley (1685–1753), see l. 123n, below.

58–64 If fear nourishes imagination (as in ll. 19–25), legends 'peopling the dark woods' will do so too. It is important that for Wordsworth and Coleridge the fully imaginative mind was inevitably a moral one 'quick to recognize . . . moral properties' (aspects or characteristics). Imagination for them was not merely creative, but led to an understanding ('apprehensive power') that would see things in their true relationship to each other, and the individual in his true relationship to the world about him.

The moral properties and scope of things.
But greedily he read and read again
Whate'er the rustic vicar's shelf supplied:
The life and death of martyrs who sustained
Intolerable pangs, and here and there
A straggling volume, torn and incomplete,
Which left half-told the preternatural tale,
Romance of giants, chronicle of fiends,
Profuse in garniture of wooden cuts
Strange and uncouth, dire faces, figures dire,
Sharp-kneed, sharp-elbowed, and lean-ankled too,
With long and ghostly shanks, forms which once seen
Could never be forgotten – things though low,
Though low and humble, not to be despised
By such as have observed the curious links
With which the perishable hours of life
Are bound together, and the world of thought
Exists and is sustained. Within his heart
Love was not yet, nor the pure joy of love,
By sound diffused, or by the breathing air,
Or by the silent looks of happy things,
Or flowing from the universal face
Of earth and sky. But he had felt the power
Of Nature, and already was prepared
By his intense conceptions to receive
Deeply the lesson deep of love, which he
Whom Nature, by whatever means, has taught
To feel intensely, cannot but receive.
          Ere his ninth year he had been sent abroad

65–81   Against the educational theorists of the day, who wanted children to
learn facts and read morally improving books, Wordsworth and
Coleridge believed that fairy stories ('preternatural tales') helped to
create a strong imagination. The 'links' that bind together 'the perishable hours of life' are not just conscious recollections, but associations
– ideas surviving in the mind that represent forgotten experience, and
connect with each other in a way that has often come to seem arbitrary.
To Hartley, who was a powerful influence on Coleridge in the mid
1790s, and on Wordsworth slightly later, it seemed that associationism
not only explained the workings of the brain, but led towards happiness
and moral strength.

72   **Profuse in garniture of wooden cuts**   richly decorated with wood-
cuts.

92   **abroad**   out.

To tend his father's sheep; such was his task
Henceforward till the later day of youth.
Oh then what soul was his, when on the tops
Of the high mountains he beheld the sun   95
Rise up and bathe the world in light. He looked,
The ocean and the earth beneath him lay
In gladness and deep joy. The clouds were touched,
And in their silent faces he did read
Unutterable love. Sound needed none,   100
Nor any voice of joy: his spirit drank
The spectacle. Sensation, soul, and form,
All melted into him; they swallowed up
His animal being. In them did he live,
And by them did he live – they were his life.   105
In such access of mind, in such high hour
Of visitation from the living God,
He did not feel the God, he felt his works.
Thought was not; in enjoyment it expired.
Such hour by prayer or praise was unprofaned;   110
He neither prayed, nor offered thanks or praise;
His mind was a thanksgiving to the power
That made him. It was blessedness and love.

    A shepherd on the lonely mountain-tops,
Such intercourse was his, and in this sort   115
Was his existence oftentimes possessed.
Oh *then* how beautiful, how bright, appeared
The written promise. He had early learned

95–114 Wordsworth is drawing on Coleridge's early Conversation Poem, *Reflections on Having Left a Place of Retirement* (February 1796), in which the poet gazing from a hilltop out to sea experiences a similar moment of pantheist communion with an omnipresent God. Lines 110–14 especially seem to recall *Reflections*, 40–2:

    No wish profaned my overwhelmed heart.
    Blest hour! It was a luxury – to be!

116 **intercourse** communication.

118–23 In 1812 Wordsworth shocked a rather conventional friend with the words 'I have no need of a Redeemer' (*Henry Crabb Robinson on Books and their Writers*, ed. Edith J. Morley (3 vols., 1938), I. 87, 158), and his sense of the God in Nature was probably at all times more important to him than the 'written promise' of the Bible. At the time of *The Pedlar*, in addition to thinking of God as a life-force permeating the natural world, he was influenced (through Coleridge) by Bishop Berkeley's view of Nature as the symbolic language of God. In the same month as *The*

To reverence the volume which displays
The mystery, the life which cannot die,
But in the mountains did he FEEL his faith,
There did he see the writing. All things there
Breathed immortality, revolving life,
And greatness still revolving, infinite.
There littleness was not, the least of things
Seemed infinite, and there his spirit shaped
Her prospects – nor did he *believe*; he saw.
What wonder if his being thus became
Sublime and comprehensive? Low desires,
Low thoughts, had there no place; yet was his heart
Lowly, for he was meek in gratitude
Oft as he called to mind those exstacies,
And whence they flowed; and from them he acquired
Wisdom which works through patience – thence he learned
In many a calmer hour of sober thought
To look on Nature with an humble heart,
Self-questioned where it did not understand,
And with a superstitious eye of love.

   Thus passed the time, yet to the neighbouring town
He often went with what small overplus
His earnings might supply, and brought away
The book which most had tempted his desires
While at the stall he read. Among the hills
He gazed upon that mighty orb of song,
The divine Milton. Lore of different kind,
The annual savings of a toilsome life,
The schoolmaster supplied – books that explain

Pedlar Coleridge wrote in *Frost at Midnight*:
      so shalt thou see and hear
  The lovely shapes, and sounds intelligible,
  Of that eternal language which thy God
  Utters; who from eternity doth teach
  Himself in all, and all things in himself.
       (ll. 58–62)

130 **Sublime and comprehensive** noble, or lofty, and well-balanced (able to take all things into account).

145 **orb** world.

148–53 At the time when Wordsworth took his Cambridge B.A. (1791) mathematics was the only subject in which the University held exams. His attitude to it varied, but in *The Pedlar* it is associated with pettiness and death of the imagination – truth in its most constricted form.

The purer elements of truth involved
In lines and numbers, and by charm severe,   150
Especially perceived where Nature droops
And feeling is suppressed, preserve the mind
Busy in solitude and poverty.
And thus employed he many a time o'erlooked
The listless hours when in the hollow vale,   155
Hollow and green, he lay on the green turf
In lonesome idleness. What could he do?
Nature was at his heart, and he perceived,
Though yet he knew not how, a wasting power
In all things which from her sweet influence   160
Might tend to wean him. Therefore with her hues,
Her forms, and with the spirit of her forms,
He clothed the nakedness of austere truth.
While yet he lingered in the elements
Of science, and among her simplest laws,   165
His triangles they were the stars of heaven,
The silent stars; his altitudes the crag
Which is the eagle's birth-place, or some peak
Familiar with forgotten years which shews
Inscribed, as with the silence of the thought,   170
Upon its bleak and visionary sides
The history of many a winter storm,
Or obscure records of the path of fire.
Yet with these lonesome sciences he still
Continued to amuse the heavier hours   175
Of solitude. Yet not the less he found
In cold elation, and the lifelessness
Of truth by oversubtlety dislodged
From grandeur and from love, an idle toy,
The dullest of all toys. He saw in truth   180

154   **o'erlooked**   neglected, failed to notice.
161   **wean**   a child is 'weaned' from its mother when she ceases to breast-
       feed it. Wordsworth's use of the metaphor here suggests a tendency,
       seen elsewhere, to think of Nature as replacing his own mother, who
       died when he was seven.
168–73   The sides of the mountain are 'visionary' – capable, that is, of reveal-
       ing truth – because they bear witness to apocalyptic events of a distant
       past. According to Thomas Burnet's *Sacred Theory of the Earth* (1684),
       which Wordsworth had been reading, the world had been made perfect,
       but then 'ruined' at the time of the Fall. The highest alpine peaks were
       thought to have been created by the retreating waters of the Flood.

A holy spirit and a breathing soul;
He reverenced her and trembled at her look,
When with a moral beauty in her face
She led him through the worlds.

      But now, before his twentieth year was passed,
Accumulated feelings pressed his heart
With an encreasing weight; he was o'erpowered
By Nature, and his spirit was on fire
With restless thoughts. His eye became disturbed,
And many a time he wished the winds might rage
When they were silent. Far more fondly now
Than in his earlier season did he love
Tempestuous nights, the uproar and the sounds
That live in darkness. From his intellect,
And from the stillness of abstracted thought,
He sought repose in vain. I have heard him say
That at this time he scanned the laws of light
Amid the roar of torrents, where they send
From hollow clefts up to the clearer air
A cloud of mist, which in the shining sun
Varies its rainbow hues. But vainly thus,
And vainly by all other means he strove
To mitigate the fever of his heart.

      From Nature and her overflowing soul
He had received so much that all his thoughts
Were steeped in feeling. He was only then
Contented when with bliss ineffable

196–201 The Pedlar is seen trying to reconcile the new science of optics,
created by Sir Isaac Newton (1642–1727), with his own experience of the
beauty of the spectrum. Compare Keats' *Lamia*, 231–3:
> There was an awful rainbow once in heaven:
> We know her woof, her texture; she is given
> In the dull catalogue of common things.

204–22 Lines that were transferred to the two-Part *Prelude* (with change of
pronoun from 'he' to 'I') in autumn 1799, and used to describe the state
of the poet's own feelings aged sixteen; see *1799*, II. 465. It should be
stressed, however, that neither in *The Pedlar* nor in *The Prelude* did
Wordsworth feel restricted to the details of his own life. In point of fact
he came to a belief in the One Life not in boyhood, but under the influence of Coleridge's Unitarianism in 1797–8, aged twenty-seven. The
time-scheme implied in *Tintern Abbey*, 66–112, is much more accurate.

205 To calm, or lessen, the feverish excitement that he felt.

206 **steeped in feeling** emotional (literally, 'soaked' in emotion).

207 **ineffable** inexpressible, unutterable.

He felt the sentiment of being spread
O'er all that moves, and all that seemeth still,
O'er all which, lost beyond the reach of thought   210
And human knowledge, to the human eye
Invisible, yet liveth to the heart;
O'er all that leaps, and runs, and shouts, and sings,
Or beats the gladsome air; o'er all that glides
Beneath the wave, yea, in the wave itself,   215
And mighty depth of waters. Wonder not
If such his transports were; for in all things
He saw one life, and felt that it was joy.
One song they sang, and it was audible –
Most audible then when the fleshly ear,   220
O'ercome by grosser prelude of that strain,
Forgot its functions, and slept undisturbed.
　　　These things he had sustained in solitude
Even till his bodily strength began to yield
Beneath their weight. The mind within him burnt,   225
And he resolved to quit his native hills.
The father strove to make his son perceive
As clearly as the old man did himself
With what advantage he might teach a school
In the adjoining village. But the youth,   230
Who of this service made a short essay,
Found that the wanderings of his thought were then
A misery to him, that he must resign
A task he was unable to perform.
He asked his father's blessing, and assumed   235

208–9　In the dominant, and surely intended, meaning of these lines, the
　　　Pedlar feels a divine presence, equivalent to Plato's World Soul, spread
　　　over the whole of the natural world. The words 'sentiment' and 'being'
　　　are not, however, capitalized in the manuscripts; and, though there is
　　　some awkwardness in the metre, it is possible to read the lines as
　　　showing the Pedlar's feeling of himself as 'being spread / O'er all that
　　　moves . . . ' Support for this secondary reading comes from ll. 102–4 of
　　　Coleridge's *France: An Ode*, written two months later: 'I stood . . . And
　　　shot my being through earth, sea and air, / Possessing all things with
　　　intensest love.'
217　**transports**　raptures, moments when the individual feels carried away.
221　**grosser prelude of that strain**　sensual experience so vivid that it is
　　　associated with the loss of bodily awareness, and creates a state of mind
　　　in which the mystical song of the One Life can be heard.
231　**essay**　attempt.

This lowly occupation. The old man
Blessed him and prayed for him, yet with a heart
Forboding evil.
             From his native hills
He wandered far. Much did he see of men,
Their manners, their enjoyments and pursuits,
Their passions and their feelings, chiefly those
Essential and eternal in the heart,
Which mid the simpler forms of rural life
Exist more simple in their elements,
And speak a plainer language. Many a year
Of lonesome meditation and impelled
By curious thought he was content to toil
In this poor calling, which he now pursued
From habit and necessity. He walked
Among the impure haunts of vulgar men
Unstained; the talisman of constant thought

237   **Blessed him and prayed for him, yet with a heart**   'As to my own sys-
      tem of metre', Wordsworth wrote in a letter of 1804, 'it is very simple:
      1st and second syllables long or short indifferently, except where the
      passion of the sense [emotion generated by the meaning] cries out for
      one in preference; 3rd, 5th, 7th, 9th, short, etc., according to the regular
      laws of the iambic.' He continues, 'This is the general rule. But I can
      scarcely say that I admit any limits to the dislocation of the verse, that
      is I know none that may not be justified by some passion or other.' As
      'the most dislocated line' he knows in his own poetry he quotes *Old
      Cumberland Beggar*, 57, 'Impressed on the white road in the same line',
      commenting: 'The words to which the passion is attached are "white
      road" [and] "same line", and the verse dislocates for the sake of these'
      (*EY*, 434). In *Pedlar*, 237, the emotion clearly attaches to 'Blessed',
      'prayed' and 'heart'. Hence the inversion of the first foot, where
      Wordsworth is normally regular (short-long) despite his quoted com-
      ment, and the fumbling rhythm of the line as a whole – intended no
      doubt to evoke the old man's anxiety.

238   **forboding**   anticipating.

239-45   The first statement in the work of either Wordsworth or Coleridge of
      the principles that underlie the Preface to *Lyrical Ballads* (1800): 'Low
      and rustic life was generally chosen because in that situation the essen-
      tial passions of the heart find a better soil in which they can attain their
      maturity, are less under restraint, and speak a plainer and more
      emphatic language.' In origin the views go back to Hugh Blair, whose
      Lectures on Rhetoric and Belles Lettres (1785) Coleridge had taken out of the
      Bristol Public Library in January 1798, just before most of the Lyrical
      Ballads were written.

251   **talisman**   the Pedlar's thoughts act as a charm that protects him.

And kind sensations in a gentle heart
Preserved him. Every shew of vice to him
Was a remembrancer of what he knew,
Or a fresh seed of wisdom, or produced
That tender interest which the virtuous feel   255
Among the wicked, which when truly felt
May bring the bad man nearer to the good,
But, innocent of evil, cannot sink
The good man to the bad.
                    Among the woods   260
A lone enthusiast, and among the hills,
Itinerant in this labour he had passed
The better portion of his time, and there
From day to day had his affections breathed
The wholesome air of Nature; there he kept   265
In solitude and solitary thought,
So pleasant were those comprehensive views,
His mind in a just equipoise of love.
Serene it was, unclouded by the cares
Of ordinary life – unvexed, unwarped   270
By partial bondage. In his steady course
No piteous revolutions had he felt,
No wild varieties of joy or grief.
Unoccupied by sorrow of its own,
His heart lay open; and, by Nature tuned   275
And constant disposition of his thoughts
To sympathy with man, he was alive
To all that was enjoyed where'er he went,
And all that was endured; and, in himself
Happy, and quiet in his chearfulness,   280
He had no painful pressure from within
Which made him turn aside from wretchedness
With coward fears. He could afford to suffer
With those whom he saw suffer. Hence it was
That in our best experience he was rich,   285
And in the wisdom of our daily life.

262   **itinerant** travelling.
264   **affections** emotions.
265–71 The Pedlar's mind preserves a balance ('equipoise', l. 268) of love. In his rather inhuman wisdom he is impartial – does not feel the bondage of being committed ('partial') to the cares and relationships of ordinary life.

For hence, minutely, in his various rounds
He had observed the progress and decay
Of many minds, of minds and bodies too –
The history of many families,
And how they prospered, how they were o'erthrown
By passion or mischance, or such misrule
Among the unthinking masters of the earth
As makes the nations groan. He was a man,
One whom you could not pass without remark –
If you had met him on a rainy day
You would have stopped to look at him. Robust,
Active, and nervous, was his gait; his limbs
And his whole figure breathed intelligence.
His body, tall and shapely, shewed in front
A faint line of the hollowness of age,
Or rather what appeared the curvature
Of toil; his head looked up steady and fixed.
Age had compressed the rose upon his cheek
Into a narrower circle of deep red,
But had not tamed his eye, which, under brows
Of hoary grey, had meanings which it brought
From years of youth, which, like a being made
Of many beings, he had wondrous skill
To blend with meanings of the years to come,
Human, or such as lie beyond the grave.
Long had I loved him. Oh, it was most sweet
To hear him teach in unambitious style
Reasoning and thought, by painting as he did
The manners and the passions. Many a time
He made a holiday and left his pack
Behind, and we two wandered through the hills
A pair of random travellers. His eye
Flashing poetic fire he would repeat

292-4   Wordsworth has in mind Isabella's references in *Measure for Measure*,
        II. ii. 118–22 to 'man, proud man, / Dressed in a little brief authority',
        who 'plays such fantastic tricks before high heaven / As makes the
        angels weep'.
295   **without remark**   without noticing.
298   **nervous**   vigorous, energetic.
318-20 Burns was Wordsworth's forerunner as a poet of everyday life, and a
        quotation from him prefaces the *Ruined Cottage* manuscript of spring
        1798 in which *The Pedlar* first appears:

The songs of Burns, or many a ditty wild
Which he had fitted to the moorland harp –
His own sweet verse –and as we trudged along,
Together did we make the hollow grove
Ring with our transports.
                              Though he was untaught,
In the dead lore of schools undisciplined,
Why should he grieve? He was a chosen son.
He yet retained an ear which deeply felt
The voice of Nature in the obscure wind,
The sounding mountain, and the running stream.
From deep analogies by thought supplied,
Or consciousnesses not to be subdued,
To every natural form, rock, fruit, and flower,
Even the loose stones that cover the highway,
He gave a moral life; he saw them feel,
Or linked them to some feeling. In all shapes
He found a secret and mysterious soul,
A fragrance and a spirit of strange meaning.
Though poor in outward shew, he was most rich:
He had a world about him – 'twas his own,
He made it – for it only lived to him,
And to the God who looked into his mind.
Such sympathies would often bear him far
In outward gesture, and in visible look,

320

325

330

335

340

> Give me a spark of Nature's fire,
> 'Tis the best learning I desire . . .
> My Muse though homely in attire
> May touch the heart.

(*Epistle to J. Lapraik*, 73–4, 77–8)

325   **the dead lore of schools**   philosophy taught as an academic discipline.

330–44   The Pedlar lives in a world of the imagination known only to him and to the God who knows his thoughts (ll. 339–41). To some extent Wordsworth's claims for this personal vision are hesitant: the natural forms may in ll. 332–5 be merely 'linked' to feeling, and the word 'found' in l. 336 does not imply that the soul was certainly there. But the use of 'sympathies' (l. 342) to characterize the affinities felt by the Pedlar suggests an overall confidence that he is not merely foisting his own emotions on an inanimate world.

334   **He gave a moral life**   he ascribed the power of acting as independent moral agents (effectively, he attributed human emotions).

Beyond the common seeming of mankind.
Some called it madness; such it might have been,
But that he had an eye which evermore
Looked deep into the shades of difference
As they lie hid in all exterior forms,
Near or remote, minute or vast – an eye
Which from a stone, a tree, a withered leaf,
To the broad ocean and the azure heavens
Spangled with kindred multitudes of stars,
Could find no surface where its power might sleep –
Which spake perpetual logic to his soul,
And by an unrelenting agency
Did bind his feelings even as in a chain.

344   **seeming** behaviour.

345–56   Instead of resting content with 'exterior forms' (l. 348), or dwelling
upon any single 'surface' or outward appearance (l. 353), the Pedlar's
eye is trained to perceive the essential – the 'perpetual logic' of existence. Because it sees through to what is permanent, it is continously
active ('unrelenting' in its 'agency'), and has the effect of regulating his
feelings, linking them into a chain of beneficial associations. The influence of the natural world upon the Pedlar's mind is beautifully evoked
in the contemporary fragment, part of which is quoted in the Introduction, pp. 17–18 above:

> To his mind
> The mountain's outline and its steady form
> Gave simple grandeur, and its presence shaped
> The measure and the prospect of his soul
> To majesty. Such virtue had the forms
> Perennial of the ancient hills – nor less
> The changeful language of their countenance
> Gave movement to his thoughts, and multitude,
> With order and relation.

In December 1801, when Wordsworth briefly attempted to extend the
two-Part *Prelude*, *Pedlar* 324–56 were adapted to go into the opening of
a third Part (see *1805*, III. 82, and 122–67).

347   **shades of difference** minute underlying differences that shade into
each other, and are thus perceptible only to an unusually penetrating
mind.

Tintern Abbey

Five years have passed, five summers, with the length
Of five long winters, and again I hear
These waters rolling from their mountain-springs
With a sweet inland murmur. Once again
Do I behold these steep and lofty cliffs,   5
Which on a wild secluded scene impress
Thoughts of more deep seclusion, and connect
The landscape with the quiet of the sky.
The day is come when I again repose
Here under this dark sycamore, and view   10
These plots of cottage-ground, these orchard-tufts
Which at this season, with their unripe fruits,
Among the woods and copses lose themselves,
Nor with their green and simple hue disturb
The wild green landscape. Once again I see   15
These hedge-rows – hardly hedge-rows, little lines
Of sportive wood run wild – these pastoral farms
Green to the very door, and wreathes of smoke
Sent up in silence from among the trees
With some uncertain notice, as might seem,   20

1   By 1804 Wordsworth himself was referring to '*Tintern Abbey*', but in print
he always gave the poem its full title: *Lines Written a Few Miles above Tintern
Abbey, on Revisiting the Banks of the Wye during a Tour, July 13, 1798*. He had
first visited the Wye Valley, in a strangely exalted state of mind (see
l. 73n, below), in August 1793.

4   In pointing to the 'inland murmur' of the Wye, Wordsworth has in mind
references in Coleridge's early Conversation Poems to 'The stilly
murmur of the distant sea' (*Eolian Harp*, 11) and 'The sea's faint
murmur' (*Reflections on Having Left a Place of Retirement*, 4).

18–23   The smoke *might seem* to tell of gypsies or a hermit in the woods, but
came in fact from iron-furnaces on the banks of the river. Wordsworth's
imagination harmonizes the scene, taking hints *en route* from William
Gilpin's picturesque *Observations on the River Wye* (1782), which he and
Dorothy may well have had with them in July 1798. 'Smoke', Gilpin
writes, 'which is frequently seen issuing from the sides of the hills . . .
beautifully breaks their lines, and unites them with the sky'; compare
the effect of the 'steep and lofty cliffs' in ll. 4–8.

20   **With some uncertain notice**   faintly discernible.

33

Of vagrant dwellers in the houseless woods,
Or of some hermit's cave, where by his fire
The hermit sits alone.
                                    Though absent long,
These forms of beauty have not been to me
As is a landscape to a blind man's eye:
But oft, in lonely rooms, and mid the din
Of towns and cities, I have owed to them
In hours of weariness sensations sweet
Felt in the blood, and felt along the heart,
And passing even into my purer mind
With tranquil restoration – feelings too
Of unremembered pleasure: such, perhaps,
As may have had no trivial influence
On that best portion of a good man's life,
His little nameless unremembered acts
Of kindness and of love. Nor less, I trust,
To them I may have owed another gift,
Of aspect more sublime: that blessed mood
In which the burthen of the mystery,

24 The 'forms of beauty' (outward shapes of landscape) have been 'impressed' as visual images on the poet's mind by the process described in *Pedlar*, 27–43.

29 **felt *along* the heart** one expects either 'felt *in* the heart' or 'felt along *the veins*'; Wordsworth's line gains its effect from condensing the two possibilities.

30 **my purer mind** often in Wordsworth 'mind', 'heart', 'soul' are used interchangeably, but in *Tintern Abbey* 'mind' is akin to 'soul', and purer (because more spiritual) than the heart, which stands for the bodily awareness that is transcended in ll. 44–7.

31–2 Compare Wordsworth's statement (to be found at *1799*, II. 364–7, though originally part of a description of the Pedlar) that the soul –
    Remembering how she felt, but what she felt
    Remembering not – retains an obscure sense
    Of possible sublimity.

39 **the burthen of the mystery** explained by the poet himself in the next two lines. Life is a burden because it is – or usually seems – a mystery, unintelligible.

38–50 The same loss of bodily awareness, and mystical communion with the life-force of the universe, is to be seen in *Pedlar*, 92–114, and, behind that, in Coleridge's *This Lime Tree Bower My Prison* (July 1797):
                        So my friend
    Struck with deep joy may stand, as I have stood,
    Silent with swimming sense; yea, gazing round

In which the heavy and the weary weight   40
Of all this unintelligible world,
Is lightened – that serene and blessed mood
In which the affections gently lead us on,
Until, the breath of this corporeal frame
And even the motion of our human blood   45
Almost suspended, we are laid asleep
In body and become a living soul,
While, with an eye made quiet by the power
Of harmony and the deep power of joy,
We see into the life of things.
                             If this   50
Be but a vain belief, yet oh, how oft
In darkness and amid the many shapes
Of joyless daylight, when the fretful stir
Unprofitable and the fever of the world
Have hung upon the beatings of my heart,   55
How oft in spirit have I turned to thee
O sylvan Wye – thou wanderer through the woods –
How often has my spirit turned to thee!
         And now, with gleams of half-extinguished thought,
With many recognitions dim and faint,
                                   60

        On the wide landscape, gaze till all doth seem
        Less gross than bodily . . .
              (ll. 37–41)

In both *The Pedlar* and Coleridge's poem the experience of sharing in the One Life comes as a direct response to the beauty of landscape. In *Tintern Abbey* there has been a surprising further development. The 'serene and blessed mood' has been experienced not at Tintern itself, but elsewhere, and as the result of visual memories stored up within the mind.

44   **corporeal frame** body ('frame' in the sense of a structure composed of parts fitted together). Compare 'bodily frame', *Michael*, 462.

50–1 There had been no room in *The Pedlar* for the thought that the belief in the One Life might be in vain. In *Tintern Abbey* the pantheist claims are still more impressive, and yet they are qualified; see ll. 86–9n, below.

53–4 **fretful stir / Unprofitable** in his use of a noun separating two adjectives Wordsworth is imitating Milton. Compare *Paradise Lost*, I, 733, 'towered structure high'.

55   **hung upon** as in ll. 39–41, Wordsworth experiences the goings-on of everyday life as a burden, something that weighs him down.

57   **sylvan** wooded (Latin 'silva').

59–62 Wordsworth feels that the picture in his mind ought to be identical to the landscape in front of him, but it isn't. Later he will come to value

And somewhat of a sad perplexity,
The picture of the mind revives again,
While here I stand, not only with the sense
Of present pleasure, but with pleasing thoughts
That in this moment there is life and food
For future years. And so I dare to hope
Though changed, no doubt, from what I was when first
I came among these hills, when like a roe
I bounded o'er the mountains, by the sides
Of the deep rivers and the lonely streams,
Wherever Nature led – more like a man
Flying from something that he dreads, than one
Who sought the thing he loved. For Nature then –
The coarser pleasures of my boyish days,
And their glad animal movements, all gone by –
To me was all in all. I cannot paint
What then I was. The sounding cataract
Haunted me like a passion; the tall rock,
The mountain, and the deep and gloomy wood,
Their colours and their forms, were then to me
An appetite – a feeling and a love
That had no need of a remoter charm
By thought supplied, or any interest

such changes as evidence of the modifying power of imagination (see especially *1799*, I. 279–87), but at this stage the emphasis is upon actuality. There would be no achievement in modifying a landscape in which the One Life could be directly perceived.

71–3   Between two statements (ll. 68-71 and 73–6) that show Nature as truly all in all, Wordsworth recollects the special circumstances of his first visit to the Wye, when he had indeed been fleeing from something that he dreaded. The previous month had been spent on the Isle of Wight, opposite Portsmouth where the British fleet was preparing for war with France. Wordsworth's political sympathies were with the French republicans (see *1805*, X. 249–74), and in addition France was the country of Annette Vallon, whom he hoped to marry, and their nine-month-old daughter Caroline, whom because of the war he had never even met. He arrived at Tintern on his way from the Isle of Wight to South Wales in a feverish and exhausted state of mind, having crossed Salisbury Plain on foot and largely without food. For an account of his strange experiences *en route* (which however cannot be entirely factual), see *1805*, XII. 312–53.

77–8   Compare *Pedlar*, 31–4, where mental images of the landscape are felt with such immediacy that they 'almost seemed / To *haunt* the bodily sense'.

Unborrowed from the eye. That time is past,
And all its aching joys are now no more, 85
And all its dizzy raptures. Not for this
Faint I, nor mourn, nor murmur: other gifts
Have followed, for such loss, I would believe,
Abundant recompence. For I have learned
To look on Nature not as in the hour 90
Of thoughtless youth, but hearing oftentimes
The still, sad music of humanity,
Nor harsh, nor grating, though of ample power
To chasten and subdue. And I have felt
A presence that disturbs me with the joy 95
Of elevated thoughts, a sense sublime
Of something far more deeply interfused,
Whose dwelling is the light of setting suns,
And the round ocean, and the living air,
And the blue sky, and in the mind of man – 100
A motion and a spirit that impels

86–9   It is extraordinary how muted Wordsworth's tones are as he moves
into his great affirmation of man's ability to perceive, and to share in,
the pantheist One Life. There is no doubt that he regards this as the
highest possible human achievement, but he looks back all the same
with regret to the earlier period when Nature could be appreciated in an
uncomplicated way, in and for herself.

89–94   Wordsworth had become sharply aware of human suffering in the
period following his stay in revolutionary France, 1791–2. As he points
out in his *Letter to the Bishop of Llandaff* (1793), it was the poor who bore
the burden of taxes raised to pay for the war. As a poet, however, he did
not see suffering merely as painful. His first great poem, *The Ruined
Cottage* (1797–8), for instance, shows it as source of deeper emotions that
are valued both for themselves, and for their power to bring out a
chastening thoughtfulness in other people.

94–103   In Wordsworth's own earlier poetry this great evocation of the One
Life should be compared not only with *Pedlar*, 204–22, (which became
1799, II. 446–64), but with the lyric of the same date, *It is the first mild day
of March*:

> And from the blessed power that rolls
> About, below, above,
> We'll frame the measure of our souls –
> They shall be tuned to love.

Behind these passages, however, lies Coleridge's Unitarian thinking of
1795–6. The concept of God as a 'presence' that 'impels' all the
elements and components of the universe (whether living or apparently
dead) comes from *Destiny of Nations*, 459–62:

All thinking things, all objects of all thought,
And rolls through all things. Therefore am I still
A lover of the meadows and the woods
And mountains, and of all that we behold
From this green earth – of all the mighty world
Of eye and ear, both what they half-create,
And what perceive – well pleased to recognize
In Nature and the language of the sense
The anchor of my purest thoughts, the nurse,
The guide, the guardian of my heart, and soul
Of all my moral being.
                  Nor perchance
If I were not thus taught, should I the more
Suffer my genial spirits to decay;

> Glory to thee, father of earth and heaven,
> All-conscious *presence* of the universe,
> Nature's vast ever-acting energy,
> In will, in deed, *impulse of all to all*!

And the best gloss on 'interfused' comes from *Religious Musings*, 420–6, where Coleridge speculates in a rather complicated way about whether God may be present in the solid matter of the universe in the form of myriads of component spirits, particles of the infinite mind,

> that *interfused*
> *Roll through* the grosser and material mass
> In organizing surge

103–8   Though he had earlier (ll. 50–1) referred to seeing into the life of things as perhaps a vain belief, Wordsworth now relates his continuing love of Nature firmly to awareness of the One Life. Because God is present as much 'in the mind of man' as in 'the living air' or 'the blue sky', it comes to the same thing in the end whether the individual perceives as an actuality, or imaginatively 'half-creates', the world of his senses. In *Lyrical Ballads* 1798 Wordsworth for some reason bothers to footnote a borrowing from the *Night Thoughts* of Edward Young (1745) – 'And half create the wondrous world they see' – but fortunately this long, gloomy, garrulous poem is not an important source, though it was then very popular.

109   **the language of the sense**   information, or stimulus, received by the senses.

112–14   Compare the double-negative transition – also felt to be rather clumsy – in Coleridge's *This Lime Tree Bower My Prison*, 45–7:

> *Nor* in this bower,
> This little lime-tree bower, *have I not* marked
> Much that has soothed me.

114   **suffer**   allow.

114   **genial spirits**   creative warmth, vitality. Wordsworth is recalling

For thou art with me, here upon the banks   115
Of this fair river, thou, my dearest friend,
My dear, dear friend, and in thy voice I catch
The language of my former heart, and read
My former pleasures in the shooting lights
Of thy wild eyes. Oh, yet a little while   120
May I behold in thee what I was once,
My dear, dear sister. And this prayer I make,
Knowing that Nature never did betray
The heart that loved her: 'tis her privilege
Through all the years of this our life to lead   125
From joy to joy, for she can so inform
The mind that is within us, so impress
With quietness and beauty, and so feed
With lofty thoughts, that neither evil tongues,
Rash judgements, nor the sneers of selfish men   130
Nor greetings where no kindness is, nor all
The dreary intercourse of daily life,
Shall e'er prevail against us, or disturb
Our chearful faith that all which we behold
Is full of blessings. Therefore let the moon   135
Shine on thee in thy solitary walk,
And let the misty mountain winds be free
To blow against thee; and in after years,

Milton's *Samson Agonistes*, 594–6:
> So much I feel my genial spirits droop,
> My hopes all flat; nature within me
> Seems in all her functions weary of herself

115–20   Dorothy, who had not been with her brother on his original visit
to the Wye, is responding for the first time to the pleasure of the scene.
In her response the poet recaptures the excitement of his own earlier
self.

122–4   Coleridge had made exactly this claim in *This Lime Tree Bower My Prison*,
59–60: 'Henceforth I shall know / That Nature ne'er deserts the wise
and pure.'

122–35   Among the most optimistic lines that Wordsworth ever wrote; he
was usually well aware that Nature was kinder to some than others.

126   **inform**   imbue, and (as a secondary meaning) instruct.

135–43   Wordsworth prays that Dorothy may live a life that is totally at one
with Nature. Coleridge in *Frost at Midnight* (the poem which more than
any other established the form and genre of *Tintern Abbey*) had conferred
a similar blessing on his infant son Hartley:

When these wild ecstasies shall be matured
Into a sober pleasure, when thy mind
Shall be a mansion for all lovely forms,
Thy memory be as a dwelling-place
For all sweet sounds and harmonies, oh, then
If solitude, or fear, or pain, or grief,
Should be thy portion, with what healing thoughts
Of tender joy wilt thou remember me
And these my exhortations. Nor perchance
If I should be where I no more can hear
Thy voice, nor catch from thy wild eyes these gleams
Of past existence, wilt thou then forget
That on the banks of this delightful stream
We stood together, and that I, so long
A worshipper of Nature, hither came
Unwearied in that service – rather say
With warmer love, oh, with far deeper zeal
Of holier love. Nor wilt thou then forget
That after many wanderings, many years
Of absence, these steep woods and lofty cliffs,
And this green pastoral landscape, were to me
More dear, both for themselves, and for thy sake.

> thou my babe shalt wander like a breeze
> By lakes and sandy shores, beneath the crags
> Of ancient mountain, and beneath the clouds . . .
>
> (ll. 54–6)

In each case, of course, the poet is reconciling himself to a sense of personal loss.

141   **mansion**   not 'a large house', as in modern usage, but an abiding-place.

145   **portion**   share, or destiny.

156   As at the end of the *Intimations Ode* –

> I love the brooks that down their channels fret
> Even more than when I tripped lightly as they

– Wordsworth asserts that more has been gained than lost by the passage of time. In each case, though, the force of the poetry has been elegiac (emphasized loss), and his exclamations are none too convincing.

THE TWO-PART PRELUDE

First Part

Was it for this

That one, the fairest of all rivers, loved
To blend his murmurs with my nurse's song,
And from his alder shades and rocky falls,
And from his fords and shallows, sent a voice   5
That flowed along my dreams? For this didst thou,
O Derwent, travelling over the green plains
Near my 'sweet birthplace', didst thou, beauteous stream,
Make ceaseless music through the night and day,
Which with its steady cadence tempering   10
Our human waywardness, composed my thoughts
To more than infant softness, giving me
Among the fretful dwellings of mankind
A knowledge, a dim earnest, of the calm
Which Nature breathes among the fields and groves?   15
Beloved Derwent, fairest of all streams,
Was it for this that I, a four years' child,
A naked boy, among thy silent pools
Made one long bathing of a summer's day,
Basked in the sun, or plunged into thy streams,   20
Alternate, all a summer's day, or coursed

---

1   'This' in ll. 1, 6 and 17 refers to Wordsworth's sense of frustration at not
    being able to get on with writing *The Recluse*, the great philosophical
    poem which had been planned with Coleridge the previous March, and
    of which *The Pedlar* was to have been a part. See Introduction, above.

8   Wordsworth quotes appropriately from *Frost at Midnight*, (l. 28), where
    Coleridge (who had been at school in London, and thought of himself
    as having been denied the full Wordsworthian childhood in Nature),
    refers nostalgically to his 'sweet birth-place' at Ottery St Mary in Devon-
    shire. Like *Tintern Abbey*, which is clearly written with *Frost at Midnight* in
    mind, *1799* may be seen as deriving from Coleridge's Conversation
    Poems, and beyond them from Cowper's *Task* (1784). The River
    Derwent runs behind the house where Wordsworth was born at
    Cockermouth.

14 **earnest** foretaste.
21 **coursed** raced.

41

Over the sandy fields, and dashed the flowers
Of yellow grunsel; or, when crag and hill,
The woods, and distant Skiddaw's lofty height,
Were bronzed with a deep radiance, stood alone
A naked savage in the thunder-shower?
　　　And afterwards ('twas in a later day,
Though early), when upon the mountain slope
The frost and breath of frosty wind had snapped
The last autumnal crocus, 'twas my joy
To wander half the night among the cliffs
And the smooth hollows where the woodcocks ran
Along the moonlight turf. In thought and wish
That time, my shoulder all with springes hung,
I was a fell destroyer. Gentle powers,
Who give us happiness and call it peace,
When scudding on from snare to snare I plied
My anxious visitation, hurrying on,
Still hurrying, hurrying onward, how my heart
Panted! – among the scattered yew-trees and the crags
That looked upon me, how my bosom beat
With expectation! Sometimes strong desire
Resistless overpowered me, and the bird
Which was the captive of another's toils
Became my prey; and when the deed was done
I heard among the solitary hills
Low breathings coming after me, and sounds
Of undistinguishable motion, steps
Almost as silent as the turf they trod.
　　　Nor less in springtime, when on southern banks
The shining sun had from his knot of leaves

23　**grunsel**　ragwort.
24　Skiddaw, due east of Cockermouth, is one of four Lake District mountains that are over 3,000 feet.
34　**springes**　snares.
37　**plied**　the boy is moving from snare to snare as a boat might ply between ports.
42–9　The guilt which led to this experience, 'not from terror free' (*Pedlar*, 27), was no doubt disproportionate, but woodcock were a luxury food, fetching as much as 10 pence apiece (£5 or more by modern standards) before being sent by stage-coach to London. They were trapped on the open fells by snares set at the end of narrowing avenues of stones, which the birds wouldn't jump over.

Decoyed the primrose flower, and when the vales
And woods were warm, was I a rover then
In the high places, on the lonesome peaks,
Among the mountains and the winds. Though mean   55
And though inglorious were my views, the end
Was not ignoble. Oh, when I have hung
Above the raven's nest, by knots of grass
Or half-inch fissures in the slippery rock
But ill sustained, and almost, as it seemed,   60
Suspended by the blast which blew amain,
Shouldering the naked crag, oh, at that time,
While on the perilous ridge I hung alone,
With what strange utterance did the loud dry wind
Blow through my ears; the sky seemed not a sky   65
Of earth, and with what motion moved the clouds!
    The mind of man is fashioned and built up
Even as a strain of music. I believe
That there are spirits which, when they would form
A favored being, from his very dawn   70
Of infancy do open out the clouds
As at the touch of lightning, seeking him
With gentle visitation – quiet powers,
Retired, and seldom recognized, yet kind,
And to the very meanest not unknown –   75
With me, though rarely, in my boyish days
They communed. Others too there are, who use,
Yet haply aiming at the self-same end,
Severer interventions, ministry
More palpable – and of their school was I.   80
    They guided me: one evening led by them

55–8 Ravens – the largest and most handsome members of the crow family,
    and still fairly common in the Lake District – were regarded as vermin
    because, like golden eagles, they were a danger to lambs. Wordsworth's
    'views' (intention) in climbing the crag may have been to claim a reward
    from the parish for destroying the eggs; the 'end' (result) was an experi-
    ence of quite another kind.
61   **amain** with full force.
77   **others** i.e., other spirits.
79   **ministry** guidance.
80   As Wordsworth puts it in the 1805 *Prelude*,
            Fair seed-time had my soul, and I grew up
            Fostered alike by beauty and by fear;
                    (I. 305–6)

I went alone into a shepherd's boat,
A skiff, that to a willow-tree was tied
Within a rocky cave, its usual home.
The moon was up, the lake was shining clear
Among the hoary mountains; from the shore
I pushed, and struck the oars, and struck again
In cadence, and my little boat moved on
Just like a man who walks with stately step
Though bent on speed. It was an act of stealth
And troubled pleasure. Not without the voice
Of mountain echoes did my boat move on,
Leaving behind her still on either side
Small circles glittering idly in the moon,
Until they melted all into one track
Of sparkling light. A rocky steep uprose
Above the cavern of the willow-tree,
And now, as suited one who proudly rowed
With his best skill, I fixed a steady view
Upon the top of that same craggy ridge,
The bound of the horizon – for behind
Was nothing but the stars and the grey sky.
She was an elfin pinnace; twenty times
I dipped my oars into the silent lake,
And as I rose upon the stroke my boat
Went heaving through the water like a swan –
When from behind that rocky steep, till then
The bound of the horizon, a huge cliff,
As if with voluntary power instinct,

Fear, however, was the more important influence. For the role of the
spirit world in *1799*, see Introduction above.

89–90   The stilted iambic rhythm – 'Jŭst līke ă mān whŏ wālks wĭth stateľy
stēp / Thŏugh bēnt ŏn spēed' – evokes the beat ('cadence') of the oars.
It is the movement of the boat which in ll. 110–14 will impart the terrifying 'measured motion' to the cliff, enabling it to rise above the nearer
hills as the boy rows out from the shore.

103   **elfin pinnace**   to the child there is a magical quality about his boat.
His pleasure in the game that he is playing, and especially the fixing of
his eyes on the horizon, makes him particularly vulnerable to the shock
that is to follow.

107–10

109   **instinct**   imbued.

Upreared its head. I struck, and struck again,   110
And, growing still in stature, the huge cliff
Rose up between me and the stars, and still,
With measured motion, like a living thing
Strode after me. With trembling hands I turned,
And through the silent water stole my way   115
Back to the cavern of the willow-tree.
There in her mooring-place I left my bark,
And through the meadows homeward went with grave
And serious thoughts; and after I had seen
That spectacle, for many days my brain   120
Worked with a dim and undetermined sense
Of unknown modes of being. In my thoughts
There was a darkness – call it solitude,
Or blank desertion – no familiar shapes
Of hourly objects, images of trees,   125
Of sea or sky, no colours of green fields,
But huge and mighty forms that do not live
Like living men moved slowly through my mind
By day, and were the trouble of my dreams.
     Ah, not in vain ye beings of the hills,   130
And ye that walk the woods and open heaths
By moon or star-light, thus, from my first dawn
Of childhood, did ye love to intertwine
The passions that build up our human soul
Not with the mean and vulgar works of man,   135
But with high objects, with eternal things,

121   **undetermined** unspecific, not pinned down.
122   **unknown modes of being** forms of life that are beyond the child's –
    presumably in fact beyond all human – experience. Wordsworth is
    being deliberately imprecise in order to evoke terrors within the boy's
    mind that cannot be defined. Compare *Intimations*, 147–8, written in
    1804 as an attempt to describe the bewilderment left behind in these
    early precious but uncomfortable memories: 'Blank misgivings of a
    creature / Moving about in worlds not realized.'
122–9 The boy's mind is not only taken over by striding nightmare forms,
    half mountain and half human, but also deprived of the reassuring ordi-
    nary mental pictures which were so important to the poet (see *Pedlar*,
    30–43).
125   **hourly objects** those present all the time – at any hour.
130–41 Wordsworth considers the feelings and thoughts of his childhood to
    have been purified because they were associated not with ordinary
    ('vulgar', l. 135) man-made things (as they would have been in a town,

With life and Nature, purifying thus
The elements of feeling and of thought,
And sanctifying by such discipline
Both pain and fear, until we recognise
A grandeur in the beatings of the heart.
Nor was this fellowship vouchsafed to me
With stinted kindness. In November days,
When vapours rolling down the valleys made
A lonely scene more lonesome, among woods
At noon, and mid the calm of summer nights
When by the margin of the trembling lake
Beneath the gloomy hills I homeward went
In solitude, such intercourse was mine.

    And in the frosty season, when the sun
Was set, and visible for many a mile
The cottage windows through the twilight blazed,
I heeded not the summons. Clear and loud
The village clock tolled six; I wheeled about
Proud and exulting, like an untired horse
That cares not for its home. All shod with steel
We hissed along the polished ice in games
Confederate, imitative of the chace
And woodland pleasures, the resounding horn,
The pack loud bellowing, and the hunted hare.
So through the darkness and the cold we flew,
And not a voice was idle. With the din,

for instance), but with the lasting and exalted ('high') objects of the natural world. Education by Nature (embodied in the spirit world of ll. 130–2) is regarded as a discipline, and 'sanctifies' ('gives a special value to' – literally 'makes sacred') the unpleasant experiences of pain and fear. The grandeur that comes as a result to be perceived 'in the beatings of the heart' may be associated specifically with fear, or more generally with human emotion. In effect this not very accessible passage is an extension of ll. 67–80. It may be seen as leading on towards Wordsworth's major statements of belief in ll. 279–96.

142–3 **vouchsafed . . . With stinted kindness** granted sparingly, or grudgingly – Nature holds nothing back.

149 **intercourse** companionship, relationship.

153 **the summons** lights in the cottage windows tell the boy that it is time to come home; he is then summoned more imperiously by the church clock tolling six.

158 **Confederate** played in groups or gangs. The placing of the adjective after the noun, and its Latin origin, both suggest that Wordsworth wants his readers to think of Milton.

Meanwhile, the precipices rang aloud;
The leafless trees and every icy crag
Tinkled like iron; while the distant hills   165
Into the tumult sent an alien sound
Of melancholy, not unnoticed; while the stars,
Eastward, were sparkling clear, and in the west
The orange sky of evening died away.
     Not seldom from the uproar I retired   170
Into a silent bay, or sportively
Glanced sideway, leaving the tumultuous throng,
To cut across the shadow of a star
That gleamed upon the ice. And oftentimes
When we had given our bodies to the wind,   175
And all the shadowy banks on either side
Came sweeping through the darkness, spinning still
The rapid line of motion, then at once
Have I, reclining back upon my heels,
Stopped short – yet still the solitary cliffs   180
Wheeled by me, even as if the earth had rolled
With visible motion her diurnal round.
Behind me did they stretch in solemn train,
Feebler and feebler, and I stood and watched
Till all was tranquil as a summer sea.   185
     Ye powers of earth, ye genii of the springs,
And ye that have your voices in the clouds,
And ye that are familiars of the lakes
And of the standing pools, I may not think
A vulgar hope was yours when ye employed   190
Such ministry – when ye through many a year
Thus by the agency of boyish sports,
On caves and trees, upon the woods and hills,

173   **shadow**   reflection, as at l. 240 below.
182   **diurnal**   daily. Compare *A slumber did my spirit seal*, 5–8, also written in
     Germany at the end of 1798:
          No motion has she now, no force,
          She neither hears nor sees,
          Rolled round in earth's diurnal course
          With rocks and stones and trees.
183   **train**   sequence, succession.
186–9   Wordsworth has in mind *The Tempest*, v. i. 33, 'Ye elves of hills, brooks,
     standing lakes and groves' as well as the 'genii' and other attendant
     spirits who are so common in eighteenth-century poetry.
191   **ministry**   guidance, agency (see l. 79, above).

Impressed upon all forms the characters
Of danger or desire, and thus did make
The surface of the universal earth
With meanings of delight, of hope and fear,
Work like a sea.
                              Not uselessly employed,
I might pursue this theme through every change
Of exercise and sport to which the year
Did summon us in its delightful round.
We were a noisy crew; the sun in heaven
Beheld not vales more beautiful than ours,
Nor saw a race in happiness and joy
More worthy of the fields where they were sown.
I would record with no reluctant voice
Our home amusements by the warm peat fire
At evening, when with pencil and with slate,
In square divisions parcelled out, and all
With crosses and with cyphers scribbled o'er,
We schemed and puzzled, head opposed to head,
In strife too humble to be named in verse;
Or round the naked table, snow-white deal,
Cherry, or maple, sate in close array,
And to the combat – lu or whist – led on
A thick-ribbed army, not as in the world
Discarded and ungratefully thrown by

---

194   **Impressed**   stamped, printed, as at l. 240 below.
    characters   marks, signs, handwriting; see *1805*, VI. 570.

198   **work**   seethe. The landscape has taken on a sort of restless activity in
the mind because so many visual images have been stored up amid the
poet's boyish sports.

208–12   Wordsworth is writing deliberately in a humorous, mock-heroic,
style derived from Cowper's *Task* and Pope's *Rape of the Lock* (1717).
Given his famous refusal in the Preface to *Lyrical Ballads* (1800) to distinguish between the language of poetry and prose, there seems to be no
reason why noughts and crosses (tick-tack-toe) shouldn't have been
'named in verse'.

215–19   The cards are old and dirty, and thickened through use ('thick-
ribbed', l. 216). Though not literally 'thrown by . . . *for* the . . . service
they had wrought', soldiers at this period were discarded without a pen-
sion after being wounded, or weakened by disease. For Wordsworth's
account of meeting one, see *The Discharged Soldier*, written in February
1798, and later included in *The Prelude* as *1805*, IV. 364–504.
    lu   the popular eighteenth-century card-game, loo.

Even for the very service they had wrought,
But husbanded through many a long campaign.
Oh, with what echoes on the board they fell –   220
Ironic diamonds, hearts of sable hue,
Queens gleaming through their splendour's last decay,
Knaves wrapt in one assimilating gloom,
And kings indignant at the shame incurred
By royal visages. Meanwhile abroad   225
The heavy rain was falling, or the frost
Raged bitterly with keen and silent tooth,
And, interrupting the impassioned game,
Oft from the neighbouring lake the splitting ice,
While it sank down towards the water, sent   230
Among the meadows and the hills its long
And frequent yellings, imitative some
Of wolves that howl along the Bothnic main.
        Nor with less willing heart would I rehearse
The woods of autumn, and their hidden bowers   235
With milk-white clusters hung; the rod and line –
True symbol of the foolishness of hope –
Which with its strong enchantment led me on
By rocks and pools, where never summer star
Impressed its shadow, to forlorn cascades   240
Among the windings of the mountain-brooks;
The kite in sultry calms from some high hill
Sent up, ascending thence till it was lost
Among the fleecy clouds – in gusty days
Launched from the lower grounds, and suddenly   245
Dashed headlong and rejected by the storm.
All these, and more, with rival claims demand

221 **Ironic diamonds** the association of dirty cards and precious stones is
     seen as incongruous. Hearts, similarly, have become so black ('sable'),
     that they resemble spades.
227 **keen and silent tooth** Wordsworth is recalling 'Thy tooth is not so
     keen' from Amiens' song, 'Blow, blow thou winter wind', in *As You Like
     It*, II. vii.
233 **the Bothnic main** the northern Baltic. The verb 'to yell' could until
     this century be used of both animals and objects, as well as human
     beings.
234 **rehearse** describe.
236 **milk-white clusters** hazel nuts. Wordsworth seems to be referring to
     the poem *Nutting*, which was written for *The Prelude*, but not included in
     any finished version.

Grateful acknowledgement. It were a song
Venial, and such as – if I rightly judge –
I might protract unblamed, but I perceive
That much is overlooked, and we should ill
Attain our object if, from delicate fears
Of breaking in upon the unity
Of this my argument, I should omit
To speak of such effects as cannot here
Be regularly classed, yet tend no less
To the same point, the growth of mental power
And love of Nature's works.
                        Ere I had seen
Eight summers – and 'twas in the very week
When I was first transplanted to thy vale,
Beloved Hawkshead; when thy paths, thy shores
And brooks, were like a dream of novelty
To my half-infant mind – I chanced to cross
One of those open fields which, shaped like ears,
Make green peninsulas on Esthwaite's lake.
Twilight was coming on, yet through the gloom
I saw distinctly on the opposite shore,
Beneath a tree and close by the lake side,
A heap of garments, as if left by one
Who there was bathing. Half an hour I watched
And no one owned them; meanwhile the calm lake
Grew dark with all the shadows on its breast,
And now and then a leaping fish disturbed
The breathless stillness. The succeeding day
There came a company, and in their boat
Sounded with iron hooks and with long poles.
At length the dead man, mid that beauteous scene
Of trees and hills and water, bolt upright

249   **Venial**   forgivable.
254   **argument**   theme, as in *Paradise Lost* (note also the use of a Miltonic *style* in ll. 248–50).
258–374   The 'spots of time' sequence is removed from its original position, and considerably elaborated, in the 1805 *Prelude*. *1799*, I. 258–79 become *1805*, V. 450–81, and *1799*, I. 288–374 are used to form *1805*, XI. 257–388. The important link-passage, *1799*, I. 279–87 is found only in the two-Part *Prelude*.
261   Though he claims to have been seven, Wordsworth was in fact nine when he went to Hawkshead Grammar School in May 1779.

Rose with his ghastly face. I might advert
To numerous accidents in flood or field,   280
Quarry or moor, or mid the winter snows,
Distresses and disasters, tragic facts
Of rural history that impressed my mind
With images to which in following years
Far other feelings were attached – with forms   285
That yet exist with independent life,
And, like their archetypes, know no decay.
        There are in our existence spots of time
Which with distinct preeminence retain
A fructifying virtue, whence, depressed   290
By trivial occupations and the round
Of ordinary intercourse, our minds –
Especially the imaginative power –
Are nourished and invisibly repaired.
Such moments chiefly seem to have their date   295
In our first childhood. I remember well
('Tis of an early season that I speak,
The twilight of rememberable life),
While I was yet an urchin, one who scarce
Could hold a bridle, with ambitious hopes   300
I mounted, and we rode towards the hills.
We were a pair of horsemen: honest James

279 Joseph Jackson, village schoolmaster from Sawrey at the further end of
     Esthwaite Water, was drowned while bathing in June 1779.
279–82 An echo of *Othello*, I. iii. 134–5, 'Wherein I spake of most disastrous
     chances, / Of moving accidents by flood and field'.
     advert refer.
282–7 A major change has taken place in Wordsworth's thinking since *The
     Pedlar* and *Tintern Abbey*. As before, the poet is concerned with visual
     memories stored up within the mind as the result of deep emotional
     response. The pictured scenes are now valued, however, not because
     they are felt to achieve a comparable permanence within the mind, but
     because of quite distinct new feelings that have come to be attached to
     them over the years.
287 **archetypes** originals (the natural scenes from which the mental
     pictures derive).
288–96 For a discussion of this famous and highly important passage –
     central in all versions of *The Prelude*, but here seen in its original position,
     and with its original implications – see Introduction, above.
290 **fructifying virtue** the power to make fruitful, or creative.
302–3 The poet, as a child of five, was staying with his grandparents at
     Penrith, and 'honest James' was no doubt their servant.

Was with me, my encourager and guide.
We had not travelled long ere some mischance
Disjoined me from my comrade, and, through fear
Dismounting, down the rough and stony moor
I led my horse, and stumbling on, at length
Came to a bottom where in former times
A man, the murderer of his wife, was hung
In irons. Mouldered was the gibbet-mast;
The bones were gone, the iron and the wood;
Only a long green ridge of turf remained
Whose shape was like a grave. I left the spot,
And reascending the bare slope I saw
A naked pool that lay beneath the hills,
The beacon on the summit, and more near
A girl who bore a pitcher on her head
And seemed with difficult steps to force her way
Against the blowing wind. It was in truth
An ordinary sight, but I should need
Colours and words that are unknown to man
To paint the visionary dreariness
Which, while I looked all round for my lost guide,
Did at that time invest the naked pool,
The beacon on the lonely eminence,

308–13   Altered and greatly elaborated to form *1805*, XI. 288–301. It is important to note that in this original version the child comes upon no positive evidence to connect the valley ('bottom') with the hanging. The gibbet, bones, and iron-case, are said to have gone – and there are many ridges of green turf on the moor whose shape is *like* a grave. Wordsworth is to be seen creating a single episode from different experiences. There had been an execution near Penrith in 1767 which the child would have heard about, but the gibbet was still standing, and there is no reason to think he was ever very near it. In the poet's mind as he writes is a quite different gibbet, a mouldered and terrifying stump which as a child he had passed every day in the water-meadows between his lodgings and the school at Hawkshead. See Introduction, above.

316   The strange, bullet-shaped, stone signal-beacon, built in 1719 to give news of Scottish invasions, is still to be seen on the hill above Penrith. The hill was not wooded in Wordsworth's day.

319–22   Compare *Tintern Abbey*, 76–7, 'I cannot paint / What then I was . . .' By heightening our sense of his difficulties, Wordsworth heightens also our sense of his achievement.

322   **visionary dreariness**   desolation so intense that it is felt to have a spiritual quality. Wordsworth probably has in mind Milton's famous oxymoron, 'darkness visible'.

The woman and her garments vexed and tossed
By the strong wind.
                    Nor less I recollect –
Long after, though my childhood had not ceased –
Another scene which left a kindred power
Implanted in my mind. One Christmas time,   330
The day before the holidays began,
Feverish, and tired, and restless, I went forth
Into the fields, impatient for the sight
Of those three horses which should bear us home,
My brothers and myself. There was a crag,   335
An eminence, which from the meeting-point
Of two highways ascending overlooked
At least a long half-mile of those two roads,
By each of which the expected steeds might come –
The choice uncertain. Thither I repaired   340
Up to the highest summit. 'Twas a day
Stormy, and rough, and wild, and on the grass
I sate half sheltered by a naked wall.
Upon my right hand was a single sheep,
A whistling hawthorn on my left, and there,   345
Those two companions at my side, I watched
With eyes intensely straining, as the mist
Gave intermitting prospects of the wood
And plain beneath. Ere I to school returned
That dreary time, ere I had been ten days   350
A dweller in my father's house, he died,
And I and my two brothers, orphans then,
Followed his body to the grave. The event,
With all the sorrow which it brought, appeared
A chastisement; and when I called to mind   355
That day so lately passed, when from the crag
I looked in such anxiety of hope,
With trite reflections of morality,
Yet with the deepest passion, I bowed low

329   **kindred power**   similar strength (a reference back to 'fructifying
      virtue' of l. 290).
340   **repaired**   went.
353   Wordsworth's father died unexpectedly on 30 December 1783, when he
      himself was thirteen; his mother had died five years earlier.
355   **chastisement**   punishment.

To God who thus corrected my desires.
And afterwards the wind and sleety rain,
And all the business of the elements,
The single sheep, and the one blasted tree,
And the bleak music of that old stone wall,
The noise of wood and water, and the mist
Which on the line of each of those two roads
Advanced in such indisputable shapes –
All these were spectacles and sounds to which
I often would repair, and thence would drink
As at a fountain. And I do not doubt
That in this later time, when storm and rain
Beat on my roof at midnight, or by day
When I am in the woods, unknown to me
The workings of my spirit thence are brought.

    Nor, sedulous as I have been to trace
How Nature by collateral interest,
And by extrinsic passion, peopled first
My mind with forms or beautiful or grand
And made me love them, may I well forget
How other pleasures have been mine, and joys
Of subtler origin – how I have felt

360   It is of course the child not the poet who believes that God has corrected
his desires. The poet values the child's emotion, which has had the
power to transform the wholly unimportant landscape into a formative
'spot of time', but he sees it for the guilty imagining that it is.

367   Scansion: ĭndĭspŭtăblĕ shāpes. There is a submerged, but interesting,
echo of Hamlet speaking to his father's ghost: 'thou com'st in such a
questionable shape / That I would speak with thee' (*Hamlet*, I. iv. 43–4).

375–6   Wordsworth is recalling a highly important passage in which Milton
describes himself as,

> Not sedulous by nature to indite
> Wars, hitherto the only argument
> Heroic deemed . . .

(*Paradise Lost*, IX. 27–9).
Both poets are defining a new subject-matter for themselves. Milton
substitutes Christian epic for the heroic battle-poetry of Homer's *Iliad*
and Virgil's *Aeneid*; Wordsworth moves on to portray a world that is
centred in the individual human consciousness.
sedulous   diligent, anxious.

375–90   In this difficult and rather pompous passage the poet stresses first
the child's unconsciousness of Nature's working: he has been diligent
('sedulous') in tracing the indirect ('collateral') interest and unrelated
('extrinsic') emotions that have caused his mind to be stocked with

Not seldom, even in that tempestuous time,
Those hallowed and pure motions of the sense
Which seem in their simplicity to own
An intellectual charm, that calm delight   385
Which, if I err not, surely must belong
To those first-born affinities that fit
Our new existence to existing things,
And, in our dawn of being, constitute
The bond of union betwixt life and joy.   390
      Yes, I remember when the changeful earth
And twice five seasons on my mind had stamped
The faces of the moving year, even then,
A child, I held unconscious intercourse
With the eternal beauty, drinking in   395
A pure organic pleasure from the lines
Of curling mist, or from the level plain
Of waters coloured by the steady clouds.
The sands of Westmoreland, the creeks and bays
Of Cumbria's rocky limits, they can tell   400
How when the sea threw off his evening shade
And to the shepherd's hut beneath the crags
Did send sweet notice of the rising moon,

     visual memories, and that underlie his continuing love. He then turns
to consider the moments when even during his boyish sports he had in
fact made a pure and direct response to the beauty of his surroundings.
The immediacy of this early period of unthinking sensual awareness
(akin to Blake's Innocence), he associates with the power of the infant
to form relationships with the world he has been born into (compare
1799, II. 267–310, and *Intimations*, stanza IX).

383   A reversal of Shakespeare's line, 'The wanton stings and motions of the
sense' (*Measure for Measure*, I. iv. 59). As at l. 375, the allusion sets up a
contrast, and is designed to assert Wordsworth's personal values.
Instinctive human emotions are portrayed by him as sacred
('hallowed') because of their primal innocence, whereas to a conventional Christian view they seem uncontrolled and a threat to morality.

385   **intellectual**   spiritual.

393–8   The poet at this time had responded with
                 a feeling and a love
      That had no need of a remoter charm
      By thought supplied, or any interest
      Unborrowed from the eye.
          (*Tintern Abbey*, 81–4)

396   **organic**   of the senses.

How I have stood, to images like these
A stranger, linking with the spectacle
No body of associated forms,
And bringing with me no peculiar sense
Of quietness or peace – yet I have stood
Even while my eye has moved o'er three long leagues
Of shining water, gathering, as it seemed,
Through the wide surface of that field of light
New pleasure, like a bee among the flowers.
　　　　　Thus often in those fits of vulgar joy
Which through all seasons on a child's pursuits
Are prompt attendants, mid that giddy bliss
Which like a tempest works along the blood
And is forgotten, even then I felt
Gleams like the flashing of a shield. The earth
And common face of Nature spake to me
Rememberable things – sometimes, 'tis true,
By quaint associations, yet not vain
Nor profitless, if haply they impressed
Collateral objects and appearances,
Albeit lifeless then, and doomed to sleep
Until maturer seasons called them forth
To impregnate and to elevate the mind.
And if the vulgar joy by its own weight
Wearied itself out of the memory,

404–8　The allusion to visual memories as a 'body of associated forms' is an explicit reference to Hartley's philosophy of 'the association of ideas', which is the basis of Wordsworth's thinking in the preface to *Lyrical Ballads*, and never far away when he is writing about the workings of memory (see notes to *Pedlar* 30–4 and 65–81, above).

407　**peculiar**　special, particular.

413　**fits of vulgar joy**　feelings of ordinary pleasure.

418–26　If, for example, one applied these terms to the final 'spot of time' (ll. 327–74, above) one might say that the association of the death of the poet's father with the wall, sheep and hawthorn bush, where the boy had waited ten days earlier for the horses, was indeed a 'quaint' one. The 'Collateral objects and appearances' of the remembered scene had been so deeply impressed by guilt, however, that the image called forth by maturer seasons caused the poet to write with entire confidence, 'And I do not doubt / That in this later time . . . The workings of my spirit thence are brought.'

426　**impregnate**　fertilize.

The scenes which were a witness of that joy
Remained, in their substantial lineaments   430
Depicted on the brain, and to the eye
Were visible, a daily sight. And thus
By the impressive agency of fear,
By pleasure and repeated happiness –
So frequently repeated – and by force   435
Of obscure feelings representative
Of joys that were forgotten, these same scenes,
So beauteous and majestic in themselves,
Though yet the day was distant, did at length
Become habitually dear, and all   440
Their hues and forms were by invisible links
Allied to the affections.
                              I began
My story early, feeling, as I fear,
The weakness of a human love for days
Disowned by memory – ere the birth of spring   445
Planting my snowdrops among winter snows.
Nor will it seem to thee, my friend, so prompt
In sympathy, that I have lengthened out
With fond and feeble tongue a tedious tale.
Meanwhile my hope has been that I might fetch   450
Reproaches from my former years, whose power
May spur me on, in manhood now mature,
To honourable toil. Yet should it be
That this is but an impotent desire –
That I by such inquiry am not taught   455
To understand myself, nor thou to know
With better knowledge how the heart was framed
Of him thou lovest – need I dread from thee

429–32 Compare *Pedlar*, 33–4, where the scenes depicted on the brain 'lay
        like substances, and almost seemed / To haunt the bodily sense'.
430   **lineaments** features.
442   **affections** feelings.
449   Wordsworth gets little credit for having a sense of humour, so it is worth
        pointing out that the over-emphasis and clumsy alliteration of this line
        is a joke against himself.
450–3   As he brings Part 1 to a conclusion with an appropriate address to
        Coleridge, Wordsworth's thoughts go back to *The Recluse*. The
        reproaches must have seemed stronger now in that the examination of
        childhood experience and the sources of adult power had tended to con-
        firm his sense of having been singled out for an important task.

Harsh judgements if I am so loth to quit
Those recollected hours that have the charm
Of visionary things, and lovely forms
And sweet sensations, that throw back our life
And make our infancy a visible scene
On which the sun is shining?

Second Part

Thus far, my friend, have we retraced the way
Through which I travelled when I first began
To love the woods and fields. The passion yet
Was in its birth, sustained, as might befal,
By nourishment that came unsought – for still
From week to week, from month to month, we lived
A round of tumult. Duly were our games
Prolonged in summer till the daylight failed:
No chair remained before the doors, the bench
And threshold steps were empty, fast asleep
The labourer and the old man who had sate
A later lingerer, yet the revelry
Continued and the loud uproar. At last,
When all the ground was dark and the huge clouds
Were edged with twinkling stars, to bed we went
With weary joints and with a beating mind.
Ah, is there one who ever has been young
And needs a monitory voice to tame
The pride of virtue and of intellect?
And is there one, the wisest and the best
Of all mankind, who does not sometimes wish
For things which cannot be, who would not give,
If so he might, to duty and to truth

1   Presumably if Wordsworth had felt able to go ahead and write the cen-
     tral philosophical section of *The Recluse*, his autobiography would have
     been shelved. As it was, Part 1 was finished shortly before Wordsworth
     and Dorothy left Germany in February 1799, and the second Part was
     added in the autumn when they were staying with the family of the
     poet's future wife, Mary Hutchinson.

3   **The passion**   the poet's unformed love for the woods and fields.

17–19   'How can anyone who remembers what is was like to be young need a
        warning ("monitory voice") not to overrate the achievement of later
        life?'

The eagerness of infantine desire?
A tranquillizing spirit presses now   25
On my corporeal frame, so wide appears
The vacancy between me and those days,
Which yet have such self-presence in my heart
That sometimes when I think of them I seem
Two consciousnesses – conscious of myself,   30
And of some other being.
                  A grey stone
Of native rock, left midway in the square
Of our small market-village, was the home
And centre of these joys; and when, returned
After long absence thither I repaired,   35
I found that it was split and gone to build
A smart assembly-room that perked and flared
With wash and rough-cast, elbowing the ground
Which had been ours. But let the fiddle scream,
And be ye happy! Yet I know, my friends,   40
That more than one of you will think with me
Of those soft starry nights, and that old dame
From whom the stone was named, who there had sate
And watched her table with its huckster's wares,
Assiduous, for the length of sixty years.   45
    We ran a boisterous race, the year span round
With giddy motion; but the time approached
That brought with it a regular desire

---

26   **corporeal frame** body. Looking back into his own past, Wordsworth
feels an awe that resembles the trance-like state of mind in *Tintern Abbey*,
44–6: 'the breath of this corporeal frame / And even the motion of our
human blood / Almost suspended . . . '

37–8   Hawkshead Town Hall (the 'smart assembly-room') was built in 1790,
faced with 'rough-cast' (a stucco of mortar and gravel), and painted
with whitewash. Lines 6–45 must be among the last sequences of the
two-Part *Prelude* to be written. They were inserted at the end of
November 1799 after the poet had visited Hawkshead on the 2nd with
his brother John and Coleridge.
   perked and flared Wordsworth's *Guide to the Lakes* shows that he
especially disliked white buildings because of the way they stood out in
a landscape.

44   **huckster** stall-keeper

45   **assiduous** attentive, industrious.

47–53 Natural beauty, though still merely an additional ('collateral')
pleasure, is beginning to be consciously valued.

For calmer pleasures – when the beauteous scenes
Of Nature were collaterally attached
To every scheme of holiday delight,
And every boyish sport, less grateful else
And languidly pursued. When summer came
It was the pastime of our afternoons
To beat along the plain of Windermere
With rival oars; and the selected bourn
Was now an island musical with birds
That sang for ever, now a sister isle
Beneath the oak's umbrageous covert, sown
With lilies-of-the-valley like a field,
And now a third small island where remained
An old stone table and one mouldered cave –
A hermit's history. In such a race,
So ended, disappointment could be none,
Uneasiness, or pain, or jealousy;
We rested in the shade, all pleased alike,
Conquered or conqueror. Thus our selfishness
Was mellowed down, and thus the pride of strength
And the vainglory of superior skill
Were interfused with objects which subdued
And tempered them, and gradually produced
A quiet independence of the heart.
And to my friend who knows me I may add,
Unapprehensive of reproof, that hence
Ensued a diffidence and modesty,
And I was taught to feel – perhaps too much –
The self-sufficing power of solitude.
        No delicate viands sapped our bodily strength:
More than we wished we knew the blessing then
Of vigorous hunger, for our daily meals
Were frugal, Sabine fare – and then, exclude

52   **grateful**   pleasing.
55   **plain**   the flat surface of the lake.
56–63   The 'third small island' on Windermere is Lady Holm, where there
        was said to have been a chapel to the Virgin Mary.
        bourn   aim, goal.
59   **umbrageous**   shady.
70   **interfused**   mingled.
78   **delicate viands**   food designed to please those with no appetite.
79–81   **Sabine**   Wordsworth is thinking of the Roman poet Horace, who had
        a Sabine farm and recommended a frugal way of life in his writing.

A little weekly stipend, and we lived
Through three divisions of the quartered year
In pennyless poverty. But now, to school
Returned from the half-yearly holidays,   85
We came with purses more profusely filled,
Allowance which abundantly sufficed
To gratify the palate with repasts
More costly than the dame of whom I spake,
That ancient woman, and her board, supplied.   90
Hence inroads into distant vales, and long
Excursions far away among the hills,
Hence rustic dinners on the cool green ground –
Or in the woods, or by a river-side
Or fountain – festive banquets, that provoked   95
The languid action of a natural scene
By pleasure of corporeal appetite.
        Nor is my aim neglected if I tell
How twice in the long length of those half-years
We from our funds perhaps with bolder hand   100
Drew largely, anxious for one day at least
To feel the motion of the galloping steed;
And with the good old inkeeper, in truth
I needs must say, that sometimes we have used
Sly subterfuge, for the intended bound   105
Of the day's journey was too distant far
For any cautious man: a structure famed
Beyond its neighbourhood, the antique walls
Of a large abbey, with its fractured arch,
Belfry, and images, and living trees –   110

84   The accounts of Wordsworth's landlady, Ann Tyson, have been pre-
      served, and in his last year at school he had sixpence a week pocket-
      money – which wasn't too bad when one considers that board and
      lodging cost only £21 a year. In January 1787 he came back after the
      half-yearly holiday with an extra guinea (21 shillings, or 105 new pence)
      in his pocket.
88   **repasts** meals.
95–7   To put it less pompously, they enjoyed the scenery more for having had
      a nice picnic.
103   **the good old innkeeper** – from whom they hired the horses.
105   **subterfuge** trickery, deception.
106–11 Furness Abbey near Barrow, is roughly twenty miles from
      Hawkshead.
108   **antique** ancient.

A holy scene. Along the smooth green turf
Our horses grazed. In more than inland peace,
Left by the winds that overpass the vale,
In that sequestered ruin trees and towers –
Both silent and both motionless alike –
Hear all day long the murmuring sea that beats
Incessantly upon a craggy shore.
      Our steeds remounted, and the summons given,
With whip and spur we by the chantry flew
In uncouth race, and left the cross-legged knight
And the stone abbot, and that single wren
Which one day sang so sweetly in the nave
Of the old church that, though from recent showers
The earth was comfortless, and, touched by faint
Internal breezes, from the roofless walls
The shuddering ivy dripped large drops, yet still
So sweetly mid the gloom the invisible bird
Sang to itself that there I could have made
My dwelling-place, and lived for ever there,
To hear such music. Through the walls we flew
And down the valley, and, a circuit made
In wantonness of heart, through rough and smooth
We scampered homeward. O, ye rocks and streams,
And that still spirit of the evening air,
Even in this joyous time I sometimes felt
Your presence, when, with slackened step, we breathed
Along the sides of the steep hills, or when,
Lightened by gleams of moonlight from the sea,
We beat with thundering hoofs the level sand.
      There was a row of ancient trees, since fallen,
That on the margin of a jutting land
Stood near the lake of Coniston, and made,
With its long boughs above the water stretched,

114   **sequestered**   hidden, remote.
118–21   The abbey in Wordsworth's day was overgrown, and partly used by
      the local farmer as protection for his animals. Several cross-legged
      knights and a handsome stone abbot are to be seen in the museum on
      the site. The chantry (l. 119) is a small chapel surviving among the
      ruins, endowed originally for the saying of masses for the dead.
132   **wantonness of heart**   *joie de vivre*, exuberance.
139   **the level sand**   one way back to Hawkshead was to ride twelve miles
      south along Levens Sands, and then take the road from Greenodd.

A gloom through which a boat might sail along
As in a cloister. An old hall was near,   145
Grotesque and beautiful, its gavel-end
And huge round chimneys to the top o'ergrown
With fields of ivy. Thither we repaired –
'Twas even a custom with us – to the shore,
And to that cool piazza. They who dwelt   150
In the neglected mansion-house supplied
Fresh butter, tea-kettle and earthernware,
And chafing-dish with smoking coals; and so
Beneath the trees we sate in our small boat,
And in the covert eat our delicate meal   155
Upon the calm smooth lake. It was a joy
Worthy the heart of one who is full grown
To rest beneath those horizontal boughs
And mark the radiance of the setting sun,
Himself unseen, reposing on the top   160
Of the high eastern hills. And there I said,
That beauteous sight before me, there I said
(Then first beginning in my thoughts to mark
That sense of dim similitude which links
Our moral feelings with external forms)   165
That in whatever region I should close
My mortal life I would remember you,
Fair scenes – that dying I would think on you,
My soul would send a longing look to you,
Even as that setting sun, while all the vale   170
Could nowhere catch one faint memorial gleam,
Yet with the last remains of his last light
Still lingered, and a farewell lustre threw
On the dear mountain-tops where first he rose.
'Twas then my fourteenth summer, and these words   175

145–8   Coniston Hall is Elizabethan.
        gavel-end gable.
150–6   They were presumably eating trout, or char, which they had caught,
        and cooked in the 'chafing-dish' (l. 153) – a portable stove containing
        charcoal.
159–61 The sun setting in the west is creating a glow over the eastern fells –
        as it quite often does.
164–5   By analogy ('dim similitude') the sunset suggests to the adolescent
        poet thoughts of death.
175–8   To describe the sentimental reflections that had passed through his
        mind as a boy, Wordsworth in ll. 161–2, 166–74, has drawn on one of his

Were uttered in a casual access
Of sentiment, a momentary trance
That far outran the habit of my mind.
     Upon the eastern shore of Windermere
Above the crescent of a pleasant bay
There was an inn, no homely-featured shed,
Brother of the surrounding cottages,
But 'twas a splendid place, the door beset
With chaises, grooms, and liveries, and within
Decanters, glasses and the blood-red wine.
In ancient times, or ere the hall was built
On the large island, had the dwelling been
More worthy of a poet's love, a hut
Proud of its one bright fire and sycamore shade;
But though the rhymes were gone which once inscribed
The threshold, and large golden characters
On the blue-frosted signboard had usurped
The place of the old lion, in contempt
And mockery of the rustic painter's hand,
Yet to this hour the spot to me is dear
With all its foolish pomp. The garden lay
Upon a slope surmounted by the plain
Of a small bowling-green; beneath us stood
A grove, with gleams of water through the trees
And over the tree-tops – nor did we want
Refreshment, strawberries and mellow cream –
And there through half an afternoon we played
On the smooth platform, and the shouts we sent
Made all the mountains ring. But ere the fall
Of night, when in our pinnace we returned
Over the dusky lake, and to the beach
Of some small island steered our course, with one,
The minstrel of our troop, and left him there,
And rowed off gently, while he blew his flute
Alone upon the rock, oh, then the calm
And dead still water lay upon my mind

earliest poems, *The Vale of Esthwaite* (1785–7) which survives only in fragments.

176   **access**   onset (glossed in the following line as 'momentary trance').

191   **characters**   letters.

208   The minstrel – remembered by Ann Tyson as 't'lad wi't' flute' – was Robert Greenwood, later Fellow of Trinity College, Cambridge.

Even with a weight of pleasure, and the sky,
Never before so beautiful, sank down
Into my heart and held me like a dream.
    Thus day by day my sympathies increased,   215
And thus the common range of visible things
Grew dear to me. Already I began
To love the sun – a boy I loved the sun
Not as I since have loved him (as a pledge
And surety of my earthly life, a light   220
Which while I view I feel I am alive),
But for this cause, that I had seen him lay
His beauty on the morning hills, had seen
The western mountain touch his setting orb
In many a thoughtless hour, when from excess   225
Of happiness my blood appeared to flow
With its own pleasure, and I breathed with joy.
And from like feelings, humble though intense,
To patriotic and domestic love
Analogous, the moon to me was dear: 230
For I would dream away my purposes
Standing to look upon her, while she hung
Midway between the hills as if she knew
No other region but belonged to thee,
Yea appertained by a peculiar right   235
To thee and thy grey huts, my native vale.
    Those incidental charms which first attached
My heart to rural objects, day by day
Grew weaker, and I hasten on to tell
How Nature, intervenient till this time   240
And secondary, now at length was sought
For her own sake. But who shall parcel out
His intellect by geometric rules
Split like a province into round and square?
Who knows the individual hour in which   245
His habits were first sown even as a seed?

228–30 The boy's love for the sun and moon is akin to patriotism and
     'domestic love' (more local feelings of pride) because their beauty
     makes him take pleasure in the region where he lives.
236   **hut** was commonly used to mean cottage (as at l. 188 above), and
     implied no condescension.
240   **intervenient** literally 'coming between'. Nature had been felt *in the
     midst* of other pleasures.

Who that shall point as with a wand, and say
'This portion of the river of my mind
Came from yon fountain'? Thou, my friend, art one
More deeply read in thy own thoughts, no slave
Of that false secondary power by which
In weakness we create distinctions, then
Believe our puny boundaries are things
Which we perceive, and not which we have made.
To thee, unblinded by these outward shews,
The unity of all has been revealed;
And thou wilt doubt with me, less aptly skilled
Than many are to class the cabinet
Of their sensations, and in voluble phrase
Run through the history and birth of each
As of a single independent thing.
Hard task to analyse a soul, in which
Not only general habits and desires,
But each most obvious and particular thought –
Not in a mystical and idle sense,
But in the words of reason deeply weighed –
Hath no beginning.
          Blessed the infant babe –
For with my best conjectures I would trace
The progress of our being – blest the babe
Nursed in his mother's arms, the babe who sleeps
Upon his mother's breast, who, when his soul
Claims manifest kindred with an earthly soul,
Doth gather passion from his mother's eye.

255–6   An envious reference to Coleridge's Unitarianism (belief in God as 'the One Life within us and abroad'), which provided him with a firm theological basis for thinking in terms of an overall harmony. See Introduction, p. 2, above.

258   **to class the cabinet**   classify sensations as if they were exhibits in a show-case.

262   Milton speaks of having to describe the war in heaven as 'Sad task and hard' (*Paradise Lost*, v. 564), and Wordsworth is tacitly claiming an equal status for his poetry about the human mind.

269–73   The first human relationship that the child forms is with his mother, and Wordsworth presents him as learning to love by seeing love in her eyes.

272   'Forms an evident relationship with another human being.'

Such feelings pass into his torpid life
Like an awakening breeze, and hence his mind,   275
Even in the first trial of its powers,
Is prompt and watchful, eager to combine
In one appearance all the elements
And parts of the same object, else detached
And loth to coalesce. Thus day by day,   280
Subjected to the discipline of love,
His organs and recipient faculties
Are quickened, are more vigorous; his mind spreads,
Tenacious of the forms which it receives.
In one beloved presence – nay and more,   285
In that most apprehensive habitude
And those sensations which have been derived
From this beloved presence – there exists
A virtue which irradiates and exalts
All objects through all intercourse of sense.   290
No outcast he, bewildered and depressed;
Along his infant veins are interfused

274–80   The mother's love is a source of energy, almost a source of life itself:
    in Wordsworth's original draft, ll. 273–4 read categorically, 'Such
    passion *is* the awakening breeze of life.' Inspired by love, the child
    becomes able to form parts into wholes, create order from his sense-
    perceptions. In effect he becomes capable of exerting the power of the
    imagination; see ll. 295–305, below.
274   **torpid**   sluggish, dormant.
280   **loth to coalesce**   unwilling to come together, make a whole.
282–4   As one might expect from *Pedlar*, 28–43 and *Tintern Abbey*, 23–50,
    Wordsworth stresses the importance – even at this very early stage – of
    the mind's ability to store up (be 'tenacious of', hold onto) visual
    images (the 'forms' received).
282   **recipient faculties**   senses.
283   **quickened**   made alive.
286   **apprehensive habitude**   a relationship in which one learns
    ('apprehends').
288–90   One should at this point be hearing *Tintern Abbey*, 101–2: 'A motion
    and a spirit that impels / All thinking things, all objects of all
    thought . . . ' The mother's 'beloved presence' (ll. 285, 288) is related by
    Wordsworth's intuition to the transcendental 'presence' of *Tintern
    Abbey*, 95. In each case there is a power ('virtue', l. 289), or life-force, that
    infuses the objects of the material world – and in each case this power
    could well be defined as love.
291–4   The child's relationship to his mother ('filial bond') is thought of as
    establishing the larger bond between man and Nature. At this period he

The gravitation and the filial bond
Of Nature that connect him with the world.
Emphatically such a being lives,
An inmate of this *active* universe.
From Nature largely he receives, nor so
Is satisfied, but largely gives again;
For feeling has to him imparted strength,
And – powerful in all sentiments of grief,
Of exultation, fear and joy – his mind,
Even as an agent of the one great mind,
Creates, creator and receiver both,
Working but in alliance with the works
Which it beholds. Such, verily, is the first
Poetic spirit of our human life –
By uniform control of after years
In most abated and suppressed, in some
Through every change of growth or of decay
Preeminent till death.
                From early days,
Beginning not long after that first time
In which, a babe, by intercourse of touch
I held mute dialogues with my mother's heart,
I have endeavoured to display the means
Whereby this infant sensibility,
Great birthright of our being, was in me
Augmented and sustained. Yet is a path

is seen as positively drawn ('gravitating') towards an earthly existence,
whereas in the *Intimations Ode* (completed 1804) the child will be portrayed as reluctant to forsake the heaven that 'lies about us in our
infancy'.

296   **inmate**   occupant; i.e., one who is fully a part of the activity of the
universe.

300–5   The sense in which the human mind may be said at once to make, and
to perceive, the external world is very complex. It is the subject of some
of the greatest poetry of the 1805 *Prelude* (see especially vi. 525–48 and
xiii. 53–119), and of Coleridge's famous definitions of the primary
imagination in chapters xii and xiii of *Biographia Literaria* (1817).

302   **the one great mind**   God.

315   **this infant sensibility**   the sensitivity, capacity for emotional
response, developed in the poet while yet an infant.

317–22   Wordsworth is taking up his story at the point where he digressed at
l. 242. His fullest account of being 'o'erpowered / By Nature' is to be
found in *Pedlar*, 185–203.

More difficult before me, and I fear
That in its broken windings we shall need
The chamois' sinews and the eagle's wing.   320
For now a trouble came into my mind
From obscure causes. I was left alone
Seeking this visible world, nor knowing why.
The props of my affections were removed,
And yet the building stood, as if sustained   325
By its own spirit. All that I beheld
Was dear to me, and from this cause it came
That now to Nature's finer influxes
My mind lay open – to that more exact
And intimate communion which our hearts   330
Maintain with the minuter properties
Of objects which already are beloved,
And of those only.
                    Many are the joys
Of youth, but oh, what happiness to live
When every hour brings palpable access   335
Of knowledge, when all knowledge is delight,
And sorrow is not there. The seasons came,
And every season brought a countless store
Of modes and temporary qualities
Which but for this most watchful power of love   340
Had been neglected, left a register
Of permanent relations else unknown.

320   **chamois**   mountain antelope that Wordsworth could well have seen in
      the Alps.
324–9   The props of Wordsworth's emotions (l. 324) are boyish pursuits that
      supported, or provided an occasion for, his love of Nature in early
      adolescence. At a later stage these 'incidental charms' (l. 237) are no
      longer needed; his love can stand on its own, and as a result he becomes
      aware of more subtle aspects of Nature's influence ('finer influxes'
      l. 328) that had earlier passed him by.
329–33   Wordsworth is claiming that there is a specially close relationship
      ('intimate communion') that may be developed only between an indi-
      vidual and the detailed characteristics ('minuter properties') of objects
      he already knows.
335   **palpable access**   an evident increase or addition.
337–42   Loving Nature for her own sake causes the poet to notice countless
      short-lived qualities and characteristics of the different seasons; as a
      result, they become registered as permanent impressions upon the
      mind, when otherwise they would have been lost ('else unknown').

Hence life, and change, and beauty, solitude
More active even than 'best society',
Society made sweet as solitude
By silent inobtrusive sympathies,
And gentle agitations of the mind
From manifold distinctions – difference
Perceived in things where to the common eye
No difference is – and hence, from the same source,
Sublimer joy. For I would walk alone
In storm and tempest, or in starlight nights
Beneath the quiet heavens, and at that time
Would feel whate'er there is of power in sound
To breathe an elevated mood, by form
Or image unprofaned; and I would stand
Beneath some rock, listening to sounds that are
The ghostly language of the ancient earth,
Or make their dim abode in distant winds.
Thence did I drink the visionary power.
I deem not profitless these fleeting moods
Of shadowy exaltation; not for this,
That they are kindred to our purer mind
And intellectual life, but that the soul –
Remembering how she felt, but what she felt
Remembering not – retains an obscure sense
Of possible sublimity, to which
With growing faculties she doth aspire,
With faculties still growing, feeling still
That whatsoever point they gain they still
Have something to pursue.

      And not alone
In grandeur and in tumult, but no less
In tranquil scenes, that universal power

343–51 There are six items in the list that follows 'hence' in l. 343: life, change, beauty, solitude more active than society (Wordsworth's quotation marks draw attention to *Paradise Lost*, IX. 249), society that is sweet as solitude, and 'gentle agitations' that derive from observing distinctions that would not normally be seen. Finally, depending on the second 'hence' (l. 350) – and still referring back to the poet's now acknowledged love of Nature – there is 'sublimer joy'.

351–71 Highly important lines, written as third-person narrative in February 1798, and transcribed in the manuscript alongside *The Pedlar*. See Introduction, pp. 17–18, above.

And fitness in the latent qualities
And essences of things, by which the mind   375
Is moved with feelings of delight, to me
Came strengthened with a superadded soul,
A virtue not its own. My morning walks
Were early: oft before the hours of school
I travelled round our little lake, five miles   380
Of pleasant wandering – happy time, more dear
For this, that one was by my side, a friend
Then passionately loved. With heart how full
Will he peruse these lines, this page – perhaps
A blank to other men – for many years   385
Have since flowed in between us, and, our minds
Both silent to each other, at this time
We live as if those hours had never been
Nor seldom did I lift our cottage latch
Far earlier, and before the vernal thrush   390
Was audible, among the hills I sate
Alone upon some jutting eminence
At the first hour of morning, when the vale
Lay quiet in an utter solitude.
How shall I trace the history, where seek   395
The origin of what I then have felt?
Oft in those moments such a holy calm
Did overspread my soul that I forgot
The agency of sight, and what I saw
Appeared like something in myself, a dream,   400
A prospect in my mind.
                              'Twere long to tell
What spring and autumn, what the winter snows,
And what the summer shade, what day and night,
The evening and the morning, what my dreams
And what my waking thoughts, supplied to nurse   405

377   The 'superadded soul' is presumably to be equated with the 'visionary
      power' of l. 360. It is neither inherent in objects of the external world,
      nor conferred upon them by the human mind, yet Wordsworth goes out
      of his way to stress its actuality.
379–83   School began at 6.0 or 6.30 a.m. at Hawkshead in the summer, so the
      walks must indeed have been 'early' (l. 378). The lake was Esthwaite
      Water, and the friend John Fleming.
390   **vernal**   springtime (adj.).
401   **prospect**   view, landscape.

That spirit of religious love in which
I walked with Nature. But let this at least
Be not forgotten, that I still retained
My first creative sensibility,
That by the regular action of the world
My soul was unsubdued. A plastic power
Abode with me, a forming hand, at times
Rebellious, acting in a devious mood,
A local spirit of its own, at war
With general tendency, but for the most
Subservient strictly to the external things
With which it communed. An auxiliar light
Came from my mind, which on the setting sun
Bestowed new splendour; the melodious birds,
The gentle breezes, fountains that ran on
Murmuring so sweetly in themselves, obeyed
A like dominion, and the midnight storm
Grew darker in the presence of my eye.
Hence my obeisance, my devotion hence,
And *hence* my transport.
                                    Nor should this, perchance,

409   **creative sensibility**   note the backward link to ll. 305–17, where the
      poet's 'infant sensibility' and the origins of adult creativity are dis-
      cussed in terms of relationship with the mother.
411–17   **plastic**   used to mean 'formative', and the 'plastic power' is
      Wordsworth's own creative spirit, or imagination. At times it is
      capricious, refusing to work according to conventional rules, but for the
      most part it is willing to be subordinate to objects of the natural world
      – prepared, that is, to enhance the effects of Nature, rather than assert-
      ing its own power.
417–25   As an 'auxiliar light', imagination seems to behave very like the
      'superadded soul' of l. 377, augmenting the power that Nature possesses
      possesses in her own right. It is subservient to Nature (ll. 415–17) in that
      it works to enhance her effects, but it is the imaginative dominance
      implied in this process that the poet chiefly values. Paradoxically it is
      because the mind is felt to be 'lord and master' (*1805*, xi. 271), that he
      gives to Nature his allegiance ('obeisance', l. 424).
425–35   As the Pedlar puts it in *Ruined Cottage*, 67–8, 'I see around me here /
      Things which you cannot see.' The 'interminable building' (though it
      sounds interminably boring) is intended to suggest the grandeur of the
      intellectual structures that can be raised upon the basis of associative
      thinking. These are more pleasing to the poet than rational analysis
      because they are constructive, whereas analysis tends to break things
      down, 'create distinctions' (see ll. 249–53, above). For Hartley's

Pass unrecorded, that I still had loved
The exercise and produce of a toil
Than analytic industry to me
More pleasing, and whose character I deem
Is more poetic, as resembling more   430
Creative agency – I mean to speak
Of that interminable building reared
By observation of affinities
In objects where no brotherhood exists
To common minds. My seventeenth year was come,   435
And, whether from this habit rooted now
So deeply in my mind, or from excess
Of the great social principle of life
Coercing all things into sympathy,
To unorganic natures I transferred   440
My own enjoyments, or, the power of truth
Coming in revelation, I conversed
With things that really are, I at this time
Saw blessings spread around me like a sea.
Thus did my days pass on, and now at length   445
From Nature and her overflowing soul
I had received so much that all my thoughts
Were steeped in feeling. I was only then
Contented when with bliss ineffable
I felt the sentiment of being spread   450

presence in the background of this passage, see notes to I. 404–8, 418–
26, above.

426–9   **that I still . . . pleasing**   the inverted word-order ('More pleasing'
would normally come before 'Than' in the preceding line) is Latinate,
and perhaps consciously Miltonic.

426   **still**   always.

428   **analytic industry**   rational analysis.

435–44   The poet aged sixteen is portrayed as having seen the world as 'full
of blessings' (*Tintern Abbey*, 135), and Wordsworth, who is about to incor-
porate one of the great pantheist sequences of *The Pedlar*, suggests tenta-
tively that he may either have projected his own feelings onto inanimate
('unorganic') objects, or truly have been able to 'see into the life of
things'. This clear central opposition is obscured because in the first
part of the sentence two reasons are given why he might have tended
towards projection: 1: the habit of associative thinking (ll. 435–6), 2. an
excess of fellow feeling (ll. 436–9).

446–64   *Pedlar*, 204–22, incorporated in the two-Part *Prelude* in autumn 1799,
with change of pronoun from 'he' to 'I'.

O'er all that moves, and all that seemeth still,
O'er all that, lost beyond the reach of thought
And human knowledge, to the human eye
Invisible, yet liveth to the heart,
O'er all that leaps, and runs, and shouts, and sings,
Or beats the gladsome air, o'er all that glides
Beneath the wave, yea, in the wave itself
And mighty depth of waters. Wonder not
If such my transports were, for in all things
I saw one life, and felt that it was joy;
One song they sang and it was audible –
Most audible then when the fleshly ear,
O'ercome by grosser prelude of that strain,
Forgot its functions and slept undisturbed.
        If this be error, and another faith
Find easier access to the pious mind,
Yet were I grossly destitute of all
Those human sentiments which make this earth
So dear if I should fail with grateful voice
To speak of you, ye mountains, and ye lakes
And sounding cataracts, ye mists and winds
That dwell among the hills where I was born.
If in my youth I have been pure in heart,
If, mingling with the world, I am content
With my own modest pleasures, and have lived
With God and Nature communing, removed
From little enmities and low desires,
The gift is yours; if in these times of fear,
This melancholy waste of hopes o'erthrown,
If, mid indifference and apathy

465–6   Compare *Tintern Abbey*, 50–8, 'If this / Be but a vain belief . . . ' It is
        noticeable that although in *1799* Wordsworth describes himself as
        coming to an awareness of the One Life aged sixteen (whereas in fact he
        had done so at Alfoxden, eleven years later), he goes on to imply that he
        is still drawn to pantheism at the time of writing.
478–86   Wordsworth is describing the political situation as it seemed to
        radicals at the end of the 1790s. Hopes in the French Revolution had
        been utterly disappointed, and those who had earlier been republicans
        were not only finding more selfish alternatives, but sneering defensively
        at people who sustained an idealist position. The passage is based on a
        letter from Coleridge of September 1799.
479   **waste** desert.

And wicked exultation, when good men
On every side fall off we know not how
To selfishness, disguised in gentle names
Of peace and quiet and domestic love –
Yet mingled, not unwillingly, with sneers   485
On visionary minds – if, in this time
Of dereliction and dismay, I yet
Despair not of our nature, but retain
A more than Roman confidence, a faith
That fails not, in all sorrow my support,   490
The blessing of my life, the gift is yours
Ye mountains, thine O Nature. Thou hast fed
My lofty speculations, and in thee
For this uneasy heart of ours I find
A never-failing principle of joy   495
And purest passion.
                    Thou, my friend, wast reared
In the great city, mid far other scenes,
But we by different roads at length have gained
The self-same bourne. And from this cause to thee
I speak unapprehensive of contempt,   500
The insinuated scoff of coward tongues,
And all that silent language which so oft
In conversation betwixt man and man
Blots from the human countenance all trace
Of beauty and of love. For thou hast sought   505
The truth in solitude, and thou art one
The most intense of Nature's worshippers,
In many things my brother, chiefly here
In this my deep devotion. Fare thee well:
Health and the quiet of a healthful mind   510

486   **visionary**   given to fantasy.
490   It is clear elsewhere that Wordsworth thought of the Romans as a
       dignified and confident people.
496–9   As Wordsworth rounds his poem off, his thoughts turn again to
       Coleridge and to *Frost at Midnight*, which he had quoted at the beginning
       of Part I. 'For I was reared / In the great city', Coleridge had written,
       'pent mid cloisters dim' (ll. 51–2).
501–5   Compare *Tintern Abbey*, 122–35.
509–14   Coleridge in November 1799 had decided to go south and become a
       journalist in London ('seeking oft the haunts of men'), whereas the
       Wordsworths were going to set up house at Dove Cottage in Grasmere.

Attend thee, seeking oft the haunts of men –
But yet more often living with thyself,
And for thyself – so haply shall thy days
Be many, and a blessing to mankind.

The fact that Dorothy in copying the poem wrote 'End of second Part' (rather than 'The End') suggests that she thought it would some day be continued, but the formal rounding-off and farewell (compare the end of *1805*), together with the fact that Wordsworth at this stage had two fair-copy manuscripts made, show that he thought of his work as completed at least for the time being. In the event he did make a brief beginning on a third Part at the end of 1801; but in January 1804, when he next took up *The Prelude*, instead of going straight on he decided to reorganize his material, and the unique features of the two-Part version disappeared. The text printed above is that of December 1799.